Designed and produced by
Albany Books
36 Park Street London W1Y 4DE

Copyright © Albany Books

Originally published in Great Britain in
1980 by Albany Books

Published in Canada by
Nelson Canada Limited, 1980

House Editor: Lynne Pegden
Art Direction: Elizabeth Cooke
Design: Malcolm White

ISBN 0 17 600803 9

Text photoset in 12/14 pt Century Schoolbook 227
by SX Composing Limited, Rayleigh, Essex

Printed and bound by Dai Nippon Printing Company Limited
Hong Kong

Jacket design: Elizabeth Cooke

Jacket photograph: Sally Anne Thompson

Endpapers: Kabardins
roaming in their native
USSR. (*Sally Anne
Thompson*)

Pages 6 & 7: New Forest
Ponies amongst the heather.
(*Sally Anne Thompson*)

Page 8: Horse and rider
take part in the second
phase of a strenuous Three-
Day Event. (*Sally Anne
Thompson*)

Black and white illustrations
on pages 36, 37, 40, 42, 43:
Annabel Milne

Extract on p.90 from
'Right Royal' by John
Masefield, reprinted with
permission of Macmillan
Publishing Co. Inc., copyright 1920, renewed 1948
by John Masefield.

The
Book of
Horses

The Book of Horses

Jane Kidd

NELSON/CANADA

CONTENTS

The Lineage of the Horse

The horse, the animal which now gives so much pleasure and excitement to spectators and riders, started its existence looking more like a rabbit. Fifty-five million years ago the horse's ancestors stood about 10 inches high. Unlike horses today, their backs were arched and their hindquarters were higher than the forehands. We have deduced their appearance from fossils alone as there were no humans around to sketch on the cave walls. These ancient fossils were discovered last century and were attributed to what was named the *Hyracotherium* (a hyrax or cony beast). They were not at that time recognized as the ancestors of the horse. When later their true status was realized a more romantic name was given – eohippus, which means dawn horse.

The eohippus of the Tertiary period lived in tropical forests. The original habitat was thought to be the south of North America, but some migrated to Western Europe via the land bridge (the Bering Straits) and much later, in the Miocene period (25–10 million years ago) more migrated to Asia and South America. It was North America, however, which was the seat of the evolution of the horse, but ironically not the home of the modern horse for the horse became extinct there about 8000 years ago. This means that there is no breed indigenous to the horse's original home.

Evolution did not progress gradually but rather in leaps, followed by long stationary periods. The most important adaptation was the result of a change in habitat – from browsing in tropical forests lush with succulent vegetation and free from the danger of predators they became grazers where ability to flee swiftly was vital for survival. The change occurred over tens of millions of years and resulted in the family of Equidae (horses, zebras and asses), animals which had adapted to an environment of open grassland rather than the rich vegetation of tropical forests.

With the change in habitat, the horse was no longer protected by trees and a relatively safe environment; the open plain offered no cover to hide behind. Flight was essential. Horses needed to grow in size, become more mobile and develop stamina. The Eohippus had normal mammalian toes (i.e. five toes on each foot) and these were gradually reduced in number until eventually there was just the middle toe terminating in a large nail – what is now the hoof. The loss of toes helped the speed and stamina requirements, but it did make it necessary to strengthen the remaining bones so that the shock could be absorbed when this smaller area landed on the ground. This led to stronger ligaments and tendons in the lower legs, but a loss of lateral movement of the foot.

At the same time the legs lengthened so that the stride could be extended and the feet and legs became lighter so that less energy was needed to lift them.

Right, above: The Przewalski horse – the only veritable breed of Wild Horse. Unfortunately, its numbers are dwindling and most, like this mare and foal at San Diego, are kept in zoos. (*Robert Harding*)

Right: The Konik is a pony with very early origins. The dorsal stripe indicates close connections with ancient breeds of horse. (*Sally Anne Thompson*)

10

Above: In Germany the horse is domestically bred except for a small herd of Dülmen ponies. There has been a good deal of cross-breeding so that there is less and less resemblance to the original types. (*London Express News and Feature Service*)

The next important change necessary for life on the plains was for teeth which could cope with the tough abrasive grass rather than lush, succulent, semi-tropical vegetation. Teeth became larger and stronger, the ones at the sides of the mouth developing elaborate patterns of ridges and folds which provided the considerable grinding powers needed for chewing. As the size of the teeth grew, the muzzle became longer to accommodate them and the neck also extended. The larger neck was needed because horses were no longer so low to the ground and their food supply still lay at their feet.

The third important evolutionary change was that they became highly sensitive to any possible dangers. Both their hearing and their vision improved, the position of their eyes moving over thousands of years from rather close to the centre of their heads to either side. This gave a wider range of vision which was much more useful than the power to see detail at close quarters. Today's horse has a very wide arc of vision spanning 215°, but a very small area on to which both eyes can focus.

Two species of wild horse have survived to modern times to give us some idea of what these early ancestors were like, but today there is only one veritable wild species – the Asiatic Wild Horse. It is also known as *Equus przelwalskii przewalskii Poliakov* because last century Colonel Przewalski of the Imperial Russian Army discovered herds of these horses roaming wild. He took some of these 12–13hh coarse-headed, thick-necked, dun ponies with short erect manes back to Russia. Some, however, are still found wild in the bleak Gobi Deserts of Mongolia but others are in zoos, with Prague boasting of the best collection.

The other wild horse, known as the European Wild Horse, the Tarpan or *Equus przewalskii gmelini Antonius*, roamed Eastern Europe and Siberia, but died out in the last century. It did so much damage to the crops of the Ukraine and the wild stallions took such a liking to the domestic mares that the last of the species were destroyed. This century the historical and scientific value of this lighter wild pony was realized and the breed has been recreated in Poland by the selective breeding of ponies that were similar to it.

There is some evidence from fossils and legend that two other types of wild horse have existed. The first is a white horse of the north tundra of Europe and Asia which was said to roam Siberia as late as 1925. The other is the prehistoric wild horse of the forests, which is said to be the ancestor of the heavy horses of Europe. Some claim, however, that these are merely local variations of the Asiatic Wild Horse and Tarpan.

The enormous range of domestic horses, from the Shire to the Thoroughbred to the Shetland, are all one zoological species and are known as *Equus caballus*. These wide variations were produced as a result of selective breeding, when man through improving the environment (feed, etc.) and through breeding from those horses which had the required characteristics, was able to produce breeds or types which suited the particular needs of the time. Thus the enormous heavy chargers of the Middle Ages were converted into the lighter and more mobile cavalry horses of the eighteenth and nineteenth centuries, and now into the even lighter and more athletic riding and competition horses of the twentieth century.

For a little over 2500 years man has been interfering with natural selection of horses and producing variations to suit his needs. He has

Above: The Thoroughbred is the horse breeder's proudest achievement. Through selective breeding it was developed into the fastest breed in the world. (*Sally Anne Thompson*)

Overleaf: The Mustangs still run wild in the USA. These are playing, however, in a more domesticated area. (*Sally Anne Thompson*)

been able to produce great changes in this relatively short period, especially in comparison to the tens of millions of years it took the horse to evolve from a forest-dwelling browser to a fleet-footed grazer on the plains.

Breeds have been developed which suit the needs of a particular country – quick, agile cow ponies in Australia, slow, strong wood carriers in Finland; and some reflect characteristics of the people – flighty, elegant Anglo-Arabs in France and powerful horses which need discipline in Germany. Countries too, have chosen different approaches to breeding; in some, such as Poland and France, the government is all powerful with enormous state studs; in others, such as England and America, it is the individuals who have had to shoulder expenses and the risk of experiments. The following is an account of how the breeds developed in each country and the systems used to achieve this.

The Middle East

The oldest pure bred in the world – the Arab – comes from the Middle East. There is some controversy as to the specific country of origin since Persia, Syria and Egypt all claim that distinction, but the strongest evidence is that it was indigenous to the Yemen in the Arabian Peninsula. The Arab is thought to come from Asiatic Wild stock and its special features – fine coat, speed, endurance – developed when it ran wild in the deserts as far back as 5000BC.

The Arab horse's first great promoter was King Solomon (974–937BC) who boasted of over 50000 horses in his stables and collected Arabs out of the desert and Egypt to fill them.

Mohammed in the seventh century used the Arab to mount his great cavalry which swept through North Africa and up into France. When finally beaten at the battle of Poitiers many of the Muslim cavalry's magnificent horses were left behind, some of which were bred to European stock to start the extraordinary influence of the Arab on the breeds in the western world.

The influence of the Arab has been as great as it has because its excellent features are prepotent (transmitted from one generation to the next) and this is probably due to the fact that their owners for centuries – the Bedouin tribesmen – practised selective in-breeding. Performance was a vital factor and only mares who had proved themselves in battles or raids could be used. Horses of alien blood were never bred from and a record of pedigrees was passed by word of mouth from one generation to the next.

Today in the Middle East the countries producing the greatest number and highest quality of Arabs are Egypt and Iran. The latter was fast developing into an important equestrian nation until the recent political disruptions. Large sums of money were being spent on the importation of racing stock and the preservation of the old Persian breeds. The most famous of the latter is the Turkoman, a breed which spread into the USSR and developed into the Akhal Teke and Iomud.

It is to be hoped that horse breeding will not decline in Iran in the same way as it did in Turkey, when the Ottoman influence came to an end in 1915, after four productive centuries. In its heyday Turkey produced excellent Arab-type horses such as the famous Byerley Turk which came to England to act as one of the three foundation sires for

the Thoroughbred. Today, however, interest in the horse is being revived and the Turks are trying to up-grade their native stock with Hungarian stallions (Nonius) to produce a new breed called the Karacabey.

Africa

North Africa is the home of a very similar breed to the Arab and one which is often mistaken for it. It is known as the Barb but is distinguishable from the more famous breed by its ram-like head and lower-set tail. The experts believe it to came from European rather than Asiatic wild stock. Today, the best examples of this old breed are found in the King of Morocco's Royal Stud.

Further south in the African continent all indigenous breeds are extinct. The most well-known breed, the Basuto pony, was developed largely from Barb and Arab stock taken to South Africa in the mid-seventeenth century.

America

Although the horse evolved mainly in America, it was extinct there by the time Columbus arrived. When Cortes invaded Mexico from Cuba he landed with sixteen horses; and the native Indians' fear for these strange creatures was so great that it helped him in his conquest of Mexico in the early sixteenth century. It was thought that Cortes brought with him some Garranos or Minho ponies, which adapted to become the Galiceño pony of today, and some larger horses of Andalusian origins. Some fell into the hands of the Indians who tended to breed for quantity rather than quality but one tribe, the Nez Percé, took pains to breed selectively. By the eighteenth century they had developed a spotted horse (useful camouflage) which became known as the Appaloosa after the Palouse River along which it was reared. When this tribe was wiped out by cavalry in 1877 the horse was taken over by the white man and is now the fifth most popular breed in the USA.

The other horse associated with the Indians was the Mustang, a horse of Spanish and Barb origins that roamed wild after escaping from the Spanish expedition to the Mississippi. Mustangs still roam, thanks largely to the government defining areas where they can run freely. In the 1950s, however, they were threatened with extinction because so many had been captured and sold for slaughter.

Like the Spanish, the British brought their own breeds, the Trotters and Thoroughbreds, when they settled the Atlantic Coast in the seventeenth and eighteenth century. These imports resulted in the Narragansett Pacer which was famous for its amble – a comfortable fast pace for long journeys. It was not fast enough, however, so it was crossed with the Thoroughbred and eventually became extinct as a breed, but not before playing its part in the development of the famous breed of Standardbreds. The foundation sire was Hambletonian 10 (1849), who was a descendant of Messenger. His stock was selectively bred and standards set (hence the name) for inclusion into the stud book. The American Trotting Register established a 1 mile speed standard: trotters have to do this distance in 2min. 30sec., and pacers (legs move in lateral, cf. diagonal pairs of trotters), in 2min. 25sec.

Above: Justin Morgan, the stallion which did everything from trotting races, to ploughing, to serving mares, and which was the foundation sire for the Morgan breed. (*Peter Newark's Western Americana*)

Right: The Argentinian polo pony. Considered the best polo pony in the world, it is bred by crossing the Criollo with Thoroughbreds. (*Jane Kidd*)

Today Standardbreds are used for harness racing, a sport which is almost as popular with American gamblers, spectators and participants, as flat racing.

The most numerous horse in the USA is, however, the **Quarter Horse**. It is also one of the oldest, having been developed by the seventeenth century settlers in Virginia and Carolina as an all-purpose horse for harness and riding work. It became much more than that – a cow pony, rodeo horse, riding, show, and a very fast race horse over short distances. The most important race for the breed is the All American Futurity, and it is worth more in prize money than the British Derby.

The other great all-round American horse is the **Morgan** which is the progeny of one extraordinary sire born in 1793 and owned by an inn keeper, Justin Morgan. When this inn keeper died the horse fell into the hands of a farmer who made Morgan's horse till the fields, haul timber, race in harness and under saddle, pull weight and stand at stud. The Morgan breed which developed from this over-worked stallion also acted as foundation stock for a breed with spectacular gaits: the three- or five-gaited Saddlebred, which was developed for the plantation owners of the South who wanted comfortable, showy animals.

At the end of the nineteenth century, Tennessee developed its own breed for similar purposes, and their Tennessee Walking Horse has even smoother gaits.

Then there are the American breeds which are defined according to colour but rarely breed true to type. These are the Palomino, the Albino and another of the Indian's favourite horses – the Pinto.

In South America the breeds are tougher, with most developing from horses of Spanish and Portuguese origins which escaped from the original settlers. They were left to roam wild and only those that were tough managed to survive. In Argentina the horse that flourished on the vast fertile Pampas is known as the Criollo. The Criollos are used in large numbers as cow ponies on the *estancias* (ranches) and when crossed with the Thoroughbred, produce the most successful polo pony in the world.

Brazil, with 9 million horses, has one of the largest equine populations in the world. Quite a percentage of the horses are the Brazilian counterpart of the Criollo, the smaller Crioulo, but there is plenty of imported stock – Arabs, Thoroughbreds and Bretons.

In Peru the Spanish settlers led a safer existence and few horses escaped, so no local Criollo developed – instead they were imported much later from Argentina. The country's famous breed is the Peruvian stepping horse or Peruvian Paso Horse with its unique fast lateral gait.

In nearly every country in the Americas, but particularly the USA, Argentina, Brazil, Chile, and Canada, flat racing is very popular. All these countries originally imported Thoroughbreds from England, but the USA in particular has produced such high quality home breds that they have become exporters of Thoroughbreds.

Australia

Australia and New Zealand relied, like America, on imported stock for their horse requirements. In the early days, more than two hundred years ago, many came from South Africa as well as South America and Europe.

The Australians' first breeding efforts were concentrated on producing a cow pony largely from Arab, Thoroughbred and Cob stock. The Waler emerged, which not only rounded up cows but became one of the most popular cavalry remounts in the world. It was only in 1971 that a stud book was formed for this stock, when it was given the grander title of Australian Stock Horse.

It was probably some of these Walers which escaped to run wild and multiply and establish herds of what became known as Brumbies – the high-spirited, sure-footed wild horses of Australia.

The Australians have developed one other breed for which they

Below: The ponies of the New Forest have a less wild habitat than most of the British native breeds. There are few hills but plenty of heather-covered areas. (*Sally Anne Thompson*)

started a stud book in 1929 – the Australian Pony. The foundation sire was the Welsh Mountain Pony, Grey Light.

The most valuable breeds in Australia and New Zealand originated in and were imported from other countries – the Thoroughbred (UK), Standardbreds (USA), Quarter Horses (USA), and Arabs (Middle East). They have, however, flourished on the lands which have proved so conducive to horse breeding, and Australian-bred stock is now exported around the world.

Asia

Horses are indigenous to Asia, with Mongolia being the home of the Asiatic Wild Horse. The Tartars bred them, Ghenghis Khan's army was mounted on them, but they very nearly followed the fate of all other wild horses, coming close to extinction. Today, as about 200 live in zoos and the government has made it illegal to shoot them, it seems likely that this breed will survive.

The working pony of China – the Mongolian – does not breed true to type and like so many of the small breeds of Asia, can be said to be 'country bred' as there are no pedigrees, stud books or selective breeding. This would also apply to the ponies of India, most of which have been influenced by some imported stock, mainly Arabs and Walers. Although the Indian ponies might not be the most elegant specimens of horsepower, the Manipur has a particular claim to fame, for it was the original polo pony. In the middle of the last century some English planters came across the game being played on Manipurs in Assam, were impressed by the game and soon it spread around the world.

The ponies of Indonesia may not be very pretty either, but they are useful. In this relatively primitive economy, consisting of more than 3000 islands, a pony which can withstand tropical heat has an important part to play in transportation and agriculture. The government is aware of this and supports breeding, but concentrates finances and administration on the Batak, encouraging the sending of the mares to Arab stallions to help upgrade progeny.

Left: The Suffolk Punch has the oldest stud of any British breed and this massive animal dates back to 1880. (*British Library*)

Below: M. Boussac's racehorse stud. French Thoroughbred stock was developed from British imports and for a century and a half the French have been successfully breeding their own. (*R. Schall, Robert Harding Associates*)

Above: For centuries the Camargue horses have roamed wild in the French marshlands after which they are named. (*Sylvester Jacobs*)

The most well-known Indonesian pony derives its fame from its unusual talent rather than from its excellence, and this is the Sumba which has long been used as a dancing pony. Bells are attached to its knees and it dances to tom-tom rhythms.

Like most Asian countries, Japan is better known for ponies than horses. The Hokkaido, which is similar to the Mongolian pony, was strong enough to be a cavalry mount. Since the economy started to boom, however, the Japanese have taken to equestrian sports and large numbers of Thoroughbreds have been imported to found a prospering racing industry and an increasing number of riding horses for competitive work.

British Isles

The mild climate and the rich soil of the British Isles is more conducive to horse breeding than Asia – horses grow larger and develop more substance. The best example of this was the development of the fastest and most valuable breed in the world – the Thoroughbred. It started

after the Restoration in the seventeenth century, when Arabs, Turks and Barbs were imported to improve British racing stock. Selective breeding over two hundred years led to a speedier, taller horse which is used in all racing countries. Although many countries tried, none could develop a horse which was faster than the Thoroughbred, so all resorted to importing British stock.

Above: France boasts of some magnificent state studs. This is the Pompadour stud which is most famous for its Anglo-Arab stock, some of which can be seen grazing here. (*Sally Anne Thompson*)

Britain's other successful equestrian exports, her Mountain and Moorland ponies, developed by natural rather than selective breeding from the types that originally ran wild in the nine areas that gave their names to the different breeds (Exmoor, Highland, etc.), and the effects that tough local conditions had on them. Today some of these ponies still run wild in their native habitats, but because of the export market, the growing number of showing classes confined to them, and the demand for their cross-breds (with small Thoroughbreds or Arabs) to act as children's riding ponies, many studs have been established.

These native ponies gave rise to a very influential, but now extinct breed – the Norfolk Trotter – which was used for most breeds of Trotters around the world (Standardbred, Orlov, French, etc.), and for today's

Above: Westphalian stallions from the German state stud of Warendorf. All the stallions of the German breeds of riding horse are regularly driven and ridden. (*Jane Kidd*)

riding horses – the Warmbloods. The Norfolk Trotter's closest relation in Britain today is the Hackney, with its eye-catching high action.

Britain's only breed of riding/driving horses is the Cleveland Bay. Bred in the district of Cleveland in Yorkshire for two hundred years, it was the farmer's all-round horse and today is most valuable when cross-bred with a Thoroughbred to produce a horse for driving, show jumping and eventing.

The heavy horses are becoming popular again after some years of being ousted from the land and roads by motorized farm machinery and trucks. Today, show classes for the largest horses in the UK – the Shires – attract many entries and spectators. They are magnificent animals which are said to be descendants of the horses William the Conquerer brought from France in 1066.

The smaller, rounder Suffolk Punch has authentic ancestors, all traceable to a horse foaled in 1760. Scotland's heavy horse – the Clydesdale – is thought to have similar ancestors to the Shire.

In Ireland the horse is a much more important feature of life than in England, and breeding is government-assisted. Ireland's work horse –

the Irish Draught – is relatively light and crossed with the Thoroughbred produces the show jumpers and eventers for which the country is
famous.

Europe

The breeders in most European countries get much more financial and
administrative assistance than their counterparts in Britain. This
might have been expected in the Communist bloc, where there is so
much state involvement, but even France and Germany channel
enormous sums into breeding fine horses. For them the horse is a
valuable symbol of prestige.

In France, government involvement began when Louis XIV set up the
Service which is now part of the Ministry of Agriculture. This government department runs 23 stud farms housing about 2000 stallions; it
organizes the stud books; distributes breeders' premiums to owners of
high-class mares and youngstock; gives a percentage of the prize
money to the breeders of horses which win races and competitions, and
heavily subsidizes prize money, riding schools and centres.

The most valuable horses in France are the Thoroughbreds, which
although originally imported from the UK, the home breds were soon
of such quality that in 1865 Gladiateur was able to cross the channel
and beat the progeny of his ancestors in the British Derby. As in
America, the second most valuable horse, the French Trotter, is used in
harness racing. This breed was developed in the nineteenth century
from Norfolk Trotters, Thoroughbreds and the French Norman mares.

These Norman mares were foundation stock to most of the French
riding horses, known now as the Selle Français. The Anglo-Arab,
systematically bred by crossing Thoroughbred, Arab and Oriental stock
from south-west France, is France's other breed of riding horse.

In Germany, the horses tend to be more pedantic than the spirited
French breeds. The heavy breeds like the Schleswig Heavy Draught do
not have the elegance of the Percheron, and the riding horses for which
the Germans are most famous are much stronger and have more equable
temperaments than the Selle Français or Anglo-Arab.

The German riding horses have had great successes in competitions
(they have won 18 gold medals, 15 silver and 15 bronze in 10 Olympic
Games), far more than any other nation's breeds. This is the result of
careful selective breeding, producing riding horses by the same scientific
principles as race horses. Most German states run a stallion stud, e.g.
Saxony runs Celle for the Hanoverian breed, Westphalia Warendorf for
the Westphalian, etc. Stallions can only stand at these studs after
passing rigorous tests; at $2\frac{1}{2}$ years they are chosen according to their
conformation, paces, pedigrees, and a veterinary examination, and at
$3\frac{1}{2}$, after at least 100 days of training, they are tested over cross-country
courses, show jumps, at dressage, weight pulling and galloping.

Mares too, are only accepted for registration if they have excellent
pedigrees and conformation; and the result is that all German breeds,
in particular the Hanoverian, Holstein and Trakehner, are in great
demand internationally.

Other European countries follow similar breeding policies to the
Germans, i.e. stallion testing and rigorous inspections before stock can
be included in a stud book. Sweden has been doing this for almost as

Above: Trakehners at stud. A breed originally developed for Frederick the Great's cavalry, they are now successful competition horses. (*Sally Anne Thompson*)

Above, right: Norwegian Fjords have roamed the rough areas of Norway for centuries but many, like these, are now bred in captivity. (*Sylvester Jacobs*)

Right, below: Lipizzaners gallop across the rough stud lands at Piber, Austria. Their original home of Lipizza now lies in Yugoslavia. (*Sylvester Jacobs*)

long as Germany and the Swedish Warmblood has been extremely successful. Before the disbandment of the Swedish cavalry (1960), the officers mounted on home breds won more Olympic gold medals than any other country.

Austria, Denmark, Holland, Belgium and Switzerland are among the countries to have adopted selective breeding policies for the riding horse since the last war. All these countries are famous for other types of breeds. Belgium was the home of the Flanders horse, renowned as the mount of the knights in the Middle Ages and as the ancestor of the internationally known heavy horse, the Belgian, or Brabant. Denmark produced the Frederiksborg, which was popular all over Europe as a carriage and riding horse but since the stud was dissolved in 1839 the breed has declined in quantity and quality. Holland rears the Friesian, a showy black horse which is one of the oldest breeds in Europe. Austria

produces the Lipizzaner, a grey horse whose ancestors were imported from Spain in the late sixteenth century to develop the most famous breed of High School horses in the world. Switzerland was more famous for her breeding in the last century when the Einsiedler, originally developed by the monks of Einsiedeln Abbey in the eleventh century, became a popular horse for troops – Napoleon imported thousands.

In Eastern Europe the two most famous horse-breeding nations are Hungary and Poland. Hungary imported a large number of horses from the UK and France in the last century to act as foundation stock for her two riding horses, the Furioso and the Nonius. Thoroughbreds were amongst these importations and flourished well enough for a Hungarian bred – Kisbér – to return to England in 1876 and win the Derby. Poland boasts today of 42 major government studs, each housing between 50 and 200 stallions. The result is that Poland has the largest horse population in Europe, about 3 million. Although a mixture of breeds are produced, including the Arab which has a world-class reputation, it is the Tarpan for which the country is most famous. These wild horses of Europe, dating back to the Ice Age, roam wild in

Below: Hungarian studs are so large that horsemen are often needed to look after such stock as these Lipizzaners. (*Sally Anne Thompson*)

the forest of Popielno. They are not pure bred but the result of collecting ponies with Tarpan features and breeding them selectively until ponies similar to the original species were reproduced.

USSR

This vast country produces an appropriately large number and variety of breeds. Forty different breed groups are recognized and all fall under strict government control. Each zone is supposed to produce two or three breeds suitable for the local climate and demands. The result is that some breeds (e.g. the Strelets), have been allowed to die out and others have been picked out for improvement with outside crosses. Examples of the latter are the Cossacks' steppe horse – the Don, and the tough Caucasian mountain horse – the Kabardin.

This scientific and rational approach to breeding has been aided by extensive use of artificial insemination, with one stallion fertilizing up to 900 mares. In addition, strict standards are adhered to, with horses between 2 and 4 years old being evaluated and classified into groups from the elite downwards.

Below: The Don horse was originally the Cossacks' horse but is now used by the Russians for all manner of activities, including driving. (*Sally Anne Thompson*)

In the USSR most of the foundation stock for the ponies is the Asiatic Wild Horse; for the horses, the Arab has played an important part. Arab tribes have lived on the borders from the earliest times; and Arab stock has always been readily available. In the last century, stock from western Europe played an important part in Russian breeding. Most of the heavy horses were based on imported stock. The Thoroughbred has been popular both as breed used for racing and to improve other breeds; and the Trotter, which is produced in large numbers in the USSR, has origins abroad. The original breed was known as the Orlov, which was the result of Count Orlov crossing an Arab stallion with a Dutch/Danish mare, but this century the Orlov did not prove fast

Breeds in the USSR are developed according to the climate, conditions and needs of the region. These have to be tough enough to feed off spartan rocky land. (*Sally Anne Thompson*)

enough so some were crossed with American Standardbreds to create the Russian Trotter.

It seems that most countries have their own particular breeds which developed largely in the wild by natural selection, and these are usually ponies. As for the horse, most breeds have been developed by man to fill one of his particular needs – carriage work, racing, trotting and now competitions. To produce the best possible horse for each discipline most countries have mixed home breds with imported stock. Consequently the breeds of the world are largely the result of very mixed marriages; the lineage of the horse is highly international.

The Horse's Physique

All horses, regardless of breed, need a basic shape and action if they are to be strong and athletic. The shape (known as conformation) and movement are characteristics which everybody involved with horses learns to recognize.

There are people who by virtue of experience and reading can quickly weigh up good and bad aspects, and are said to have 'an eye for a horse'. Even these experts, however, cannot be sure about internal and potential problems (arising from the heart, lungs, eyes and bone structure). A veterinary surgeon and sometimes X-rays are needed to complete a thorough examination.

The physical features of a horse will be examined critically in this chapter to give the reader an idea of what to look for.

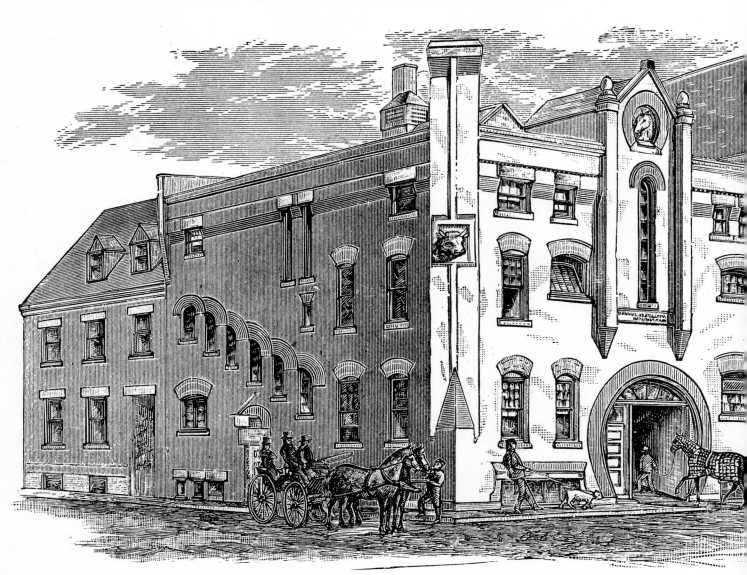

Sex

When one is initially confronted with a horse the first feature to examine is its sex. Although sex doesn't affect ability, it can make a marked difference to the horse's character and its suitability for different riders or drivers.

The real gentlemen – the stallions – are usually the most intelligent, have the greatest showmanship ('presence'), but are also the most wayward. They need firm, competent handling if they are not to learn bad habits rather than good. Outside stud work the stallion is rarely suitable for general equestrian activities unless he is under the control of a high-class horseman. In flat racing, the one equestrian sport where the stallion is commonly used, his career is effectively over by the time he is five years old. At this age all stallions except those with exceptionally good temperaments are retired to stud.

Mares have difficult temperaments too, usually showing such traits as changeable moods, sensitivity and nervousness. Many dealers and strong horsemen will not touch mares because they find them unreliable, but mares can be won over. When they are in the hands of a patient, sympathetic rider who persuades rather than disciplines, they will try far harder than their stallion counterparts. Mares may be temperamental but their ability can be increased by tactful horsemen.

A gelding is an emasculated horse – a colt (young stallion) that has been castrated usually between one and two years old. Geldings generally have kinder, easier temperaments than mares or stallions and are the most popular horses with the majority of riders.

Height

The height of a horse determines how appropriate it is for the person and/or purpose for which it is required. A very tall horse, for example, needs a well-built rider to control it and would be unlikely to make a carriage horse.

The height of the horse is defined as the distance between the horse's withers and the ground. In English-speaking countries this is measured in 'hands', each hand being four inches, so that a horse will be referred to as X hands high, abbreviated to hh. In other countries it is measured in centimetres.

The division between horses and ponies is at 14.2hh (144cm): those under this height are ponies and those above horses. Although ponies are used mainly by children the stockier versions can carry adults and most are capable of transporting heavier loads as they can pull greater weights in a carriage than they can carry upon their backs.

Colour

When there is an opportunity to choose the colour those people who are wary of high-spirited horses should avoid blacks and light chestnuts (a yellowish colour). The most popular colours are bays (brownish with a black mane and tail), darker chestnuts/sorrel (ginger, yellowish), browns (dark brown to black) and greys (white to dark grey).

For those who like eye-catching horses the palominos (golden with flaxen mane and tail) are the flashiest although the pintos – the piebald

Below: A veterinary surgeon needs a long training to acquire the necessary knowledge. This is one of the earliest veterinary schools at Harvard, Boston, USA. It was built in 1885. (*Peter Newark's Western Americana*)

34

(large irregular patches of black and white) or skewbald (large patches of white with any colour but black) – are also decorative.

Then there are the less usual colours – the duns, which are either blue dun (diluted black with black points) or yellow dun (yellowish on black skin with black mane and tail), and the roans which are either blue roan (black or brown with a sprinkling of white hairs) or strawberry/chestnut (chestnut with the same sprinkling of white hairs).

Except for the pintos most horses have patches of white hair which are referred to as their markings. On the face a small area of white above or between the eyes is known as a star; a line from the forehead to the nostrils as a stripe, when it is wider as a blaze and when wider still as a white face. If the white patch is between the nostrils then it is known as a snip. On the legs, if there is a small white patch extending only a few inches above the hoof, then it is a sock, but if it reaches as far as the knee then it is a stocking. Stripes on the body (usually in black) are known as zebra markings.

Age

The life-span and maturity of a horse will vary from breed to breed. The Thoroughbred, for example, matures early and is ready for work on the racecourse at two years of age. The majority of riding horses, however, have to carry heavier weights than the miniscule race jockey; thus they will not be broken in (taught to accept control by the rider) until three years of age or put into full work until four or five years.

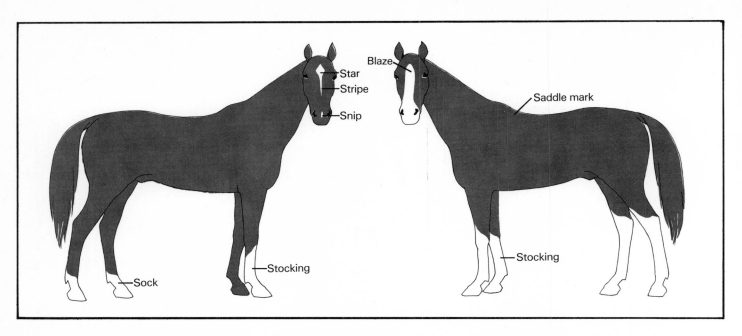

Above: The horse's markings.

The working career of most horses lasts until they are between thirteen and sixteen years of age, after which few can do more than breed, go for gentle hacks or live a life of idleness in the fields.

It is therefore vital when purchasing a horse to be able to age it, for unscrupulous dealers will sell two-year-olds as 'just ready for a good season's hunting' or seventeen-year-olds as 'the right type to start some show jumping'. Pure breds should have registration papers including their date of birth which solves the problem of ageing, but many riding horses and ponies are not registered, and that is when the teeth have to be examined.

When assessing a horse's age from its teeth until it is $4\frac{1}{2}$ years old, reference is made to the development of the six incisors (front teeth) as they change from deciduous (milk) teeth to permanent. At $2\frac{1}{2}$ years the pair of central incisors change, at $3\frac{1}{2}$ years the pair of lateral incisors erupt, and at $4\frac{1}{2}$ years the corner incisors. After this the horse's age can be assessed by the wear of the teeth, for both the profile (looked at from the side of the mouth), which gradually changes from vertical to nearly horizontal, and the flat table of the teeth, which changes from oval to circular to triangular, will help the experienced judge to make an accurate assessment up to eight years of age and a good estimate after this.

Conformation

A horse with good conformation is one which has a serviceable shape which gives it the strength and manoeuvrability to stand up to the rigours of life. It will usually be a better athlete and more likely to remain sound as there are none (or few) of those weak areas in limb and body which reduce flexibility and are liable to strain.

The first important factor in a study of the conformation is the impact the horse makes upon the initial viewing. The horse should be in proportion and the effect harmonious. Short, thin legs and a heavy, big body are not only ugly but often point to the likelihood of the horse going lame as the limbs will not be strong enough to give the necessary support.

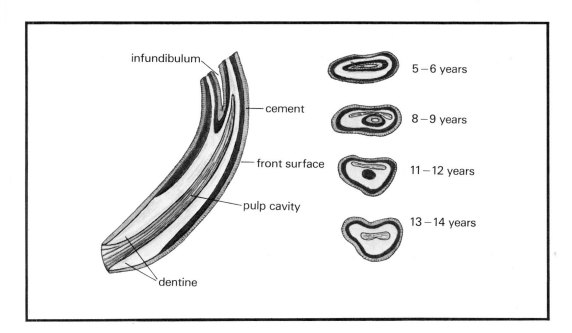

infundibulum

cement

front surface

pulp cavity

dentine

5 – 6 years

8 – 9 years

11 – 12 years

13 – 14 years

Left: Diagrams of the longitudinal and transverse sections of the teeth.

Below: Points of a horse. (*Sally Anne Thompson*)

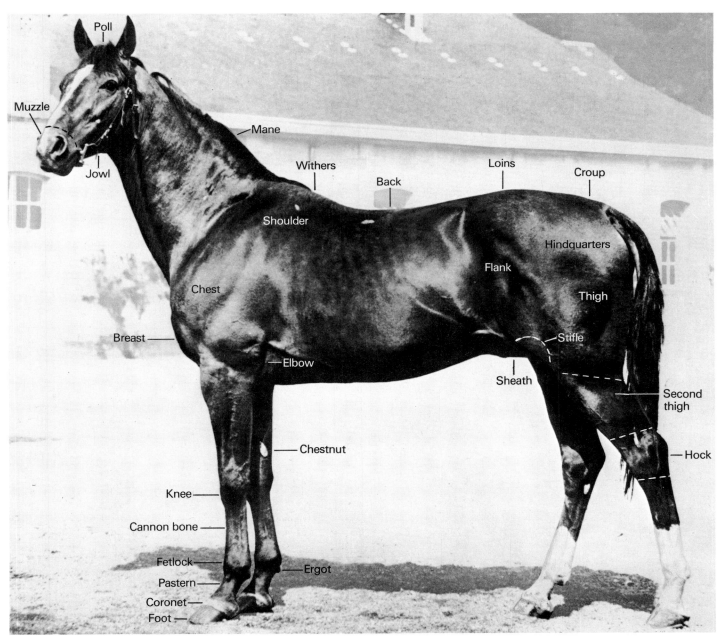

Poll

Muzzle

Jowl

Mane

Withers

Back

Loins

Croup

Shoulder

Hindquarters

Flank

Chest

Thigh

Breast

Stifle

Elbow

Sheath

Second thigh

Chestnut

Hock

Knee

Cannon bone

Fetlock

Ergot

Pastern

Coronet

Foot

The examination then passes on to the front end of the horse – the head, neck and shoulders which are known as the 'forehand'. The head is one of the best indicators of the horse's character. Broad based, largish alert ears and round, bold eyes set wide apart are usually found only on horses with kind, generous natures. On the other hand, small ears which are often laid back, and nervously flashing eyes especially with white around them, are signs that the horse is a spirited, temperamental animal.

The head is also an indicator of breeding, for when it is elegant with a straight to slightly dished profile, then the horse is usually a member of the upper equine classes like the Arabs or Thoroughbreds. Such a horse is likely to have more energy and a less docile nature than one with a plainer, larger head which verges towards or has a convex profile. Those riders who are searching for a brilliant animal should choose one with the distinguished head but those who want a calm, easy ride would generally be wiser to select one with a more common head.

The most beautiful necks are relatively long with an arched (convex) top line. Such a neck is more powerful and will give the rider a feeling of security with so much of the horse in front of him when he is in the saddle. Necks help the horse to balance himself and short necks have less scope to perform this vital function than longer versions. The worst type of short neck is one with a concave top line – known as a ewe neck. This is ugly and as all the muscles are on the underside of the neck the head carriage tends to be high, and the horse's movement very stiff.

The manner in which the head joins the neck is also important for if the poll and jowl are far apart then the horse will have to crease his windpipe in order to flex and carry his head correctly. This flaw in the conformation usually leads to wind problems.

The shape of the shoulder affects the movement of the forelegs. Thus a long sloping shoulder enables a horse to take free sweeping strides (best for a riding horse), whereas an upright (more vertical) shoulder restricts the length of its strides but gives the horse more pulling power – a characteristic that is ideal for carriage horses.

It is important that the width between the left and right shoulders should be sufficient to enable the forelegs to operate freely and to give room for the chest which contains the heart and lungs. The more space there is for these vital organs, the greater the horse's capacity for endurance; as a result horsemen look for deep as well as broad chests. A deep chest means there is a good distance between the horse's withers and the point of his elbow, so that he will need a long girth to secure his saddle. For this reason a horse which has a deep, broad chest is often referred to as having a good girth.

The back bears the weight of the rider and it is therefore of vital importance. A very short back may be strong but it tends to be rather stiff; a very long back may be comfortable for the rider as it is usually more supple, but the length weakens it and makes it more liable to develop problems. The compromise – neither too long or short a back – is the ideal.

The shape of this weight-bearing area is also important. The top line should be just concave, for both a convex shape (known as a roach back) and too hollow a back are less supple and strong.

The hindquarters are the source of the horse's power. It is the muscles

Right: A skewbald pony. These two-coloured horses are usually half-breds. Few of the pure-breds have such spectacular patches. (*Sally Anne Thompson*)

Below, right: The Thoroughbred is the fastest and most spirited breed of horse in the world. It is most suitable for riding where speed and stamina are important and needs tactful riders who are not too heavy. (*Sally Anne Thompson*)

Right: A ewe neck.

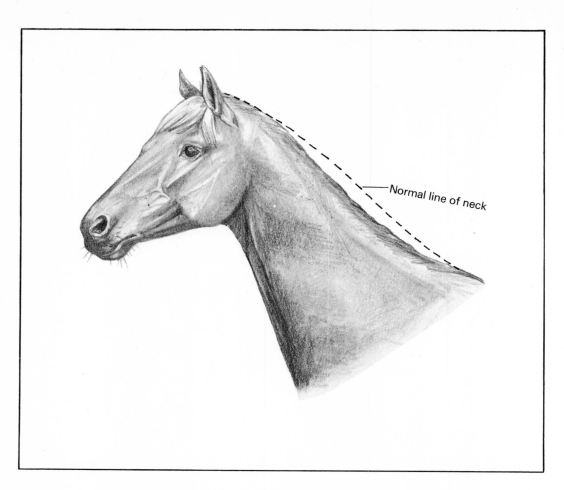

Normal line of neck

in this area which enable the horse to spring into the air, to gallop and to perform the complicated dressage movements. It is important that the hindquarters should be relatively large to give the muscles the space to develop, and they should have a longish, rounded top line which neither falls away sharply to the tail or is short and flat.

The horse's head and body are examined mainly to ascertain its character, strength and mobility. The horse's limbs, however, are examined as potential areas of lameness. The limbs have to carry the body and the strain thus incurred means that only an exceptional horse will never have leg problems. Most have frequent troubles in these areas, especially as they grow older.

The forelegs are the first to hit the ground and therefore have to absorb considerable concussion, especially when a horse gallops or jumps a fence. Consequently they are the most common sources of lameness. Ideally the forelegs should be almost straight from the fore-arm to the pastern and then the latter should slope gently towards the foot. The knees should be neither turned in or bowed out, and similarly the feet should point straight forward: if they are turned out or inwards they place extra strain on the joints.

The knee should be quite flat. It is better, however, to have a convex outline (known as over at the knee) than a concave one (behind at the knee), for the latter places far greater strain on the tendons than the former.

The circumference of the leg just below the knee is known as the horse's 'bone'. It is an indication of the horse's weight-carrying capacity as the more bone there is the greater his strength, especially if it is flat, dense bone.

The fetlocks are an important area of articulation and a frequent source of problems. They are strongest if not too rounded or narrow but flat and well-defined.

The pasterns, which run from the fetlocks to the feet, act as the rider's cushions. If this region is long and sloping it allows the fetlock to move towards the ground and softens the jar as the foot hits the ground. This movement, however, puts strain on the tendons and although comfortable for the rider can create lameness. On the other hand, short, upright pasterns are relatively immobile so that the jar upon landing is great, the ride uncomfortable and the poor shock absorption often creates problems in the joints and feet. The ideal is again a compromise – neither too long or too short pasterns.

The foot at the base of the limb is an important shock absorber. The best shape for this purpose is a round, open hoof, so that there is a relatively large area to absorb the impact. Small, narrow (known as boxy) feet should be avoided and large, flat feet tend to be cumbersome.

The pairs of feet should be symmetrical so that they can share the work evenly. Their surfaces should be smooth and strong, without cracks or rings.

The forelimbs absorb the impact upon hitting the ground, but the hind limbs are more important as sources of the power enabling the horse to spring into the air and to take bouncy strides. Much of this power comes from the second thigh, which should be muscular and quite long, and from the hocks.

The hocks should be quite wide from front to back and the bone that forms them should be well-defined without protruding too far. The hock should have a lean covering of flesh, and any puffiness is usually a sign

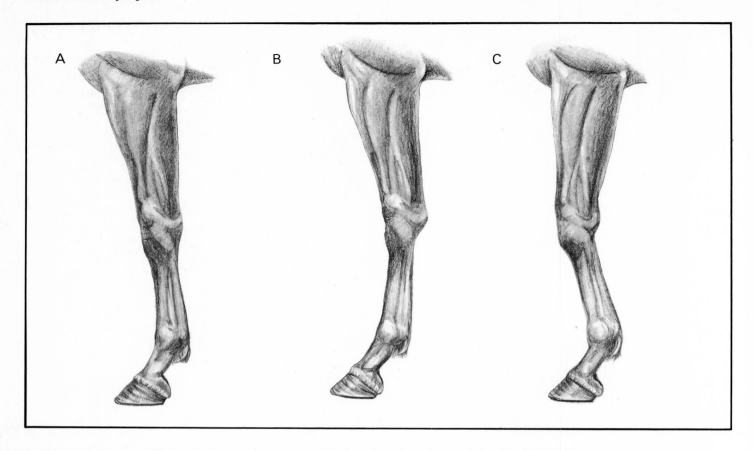

Above: Good and bad
forelegs
a) Good foreleg
b) Back at the knee
c) Over at the knee

of strain. When viewed from the rear the hocks should neither point inwards (known as cow hocks) or outwards (bowed hocks). Seen in profile the hocks should not be too concave or sickle-shaped (known as sickle hocks); but hocks which are very straight restrict the movement in the joints and so prevent the hind leg from taking long, active strides. Hocks which compromise between these extremes are the strongest.

Movement

Sex, height, age, colour and conformation can all be examined when the horse is standing still, but most of the time he will be on the move so a study of his action is vital. Most horses have three basic paces/gaits – the walk, trot and canter; the gallop is an extension of the canter. There are, however, some breeds which inherit and/or are capable of being trained to perform rather more unusual gaits. America is the most common breeding ground for these variations: Saddlebreds and Tennessee Walkers are some of the most popular multi-gaited breeds. Their unusual paces have been discussed earlier.

Of the paces/gaits the one which every breed or type should perform the slowest is the walk. At this gait four hoof beats are heard with the horse moving one leg after another. The sequence is right hind leg, right foreleg, left hind leg, left foreleg. This is a comfortable pace for the rider as there are always two or three legs on the ground; the horse does not spring into the air for a moment of suspension as in the faster gait – the trot.

In the trot (which is known as the jog by Western riders), just two hoof beats are heard, with the horse moving his legs in diagonal pairs. The sequence is right foreleg and left hind leg leave the ground, left

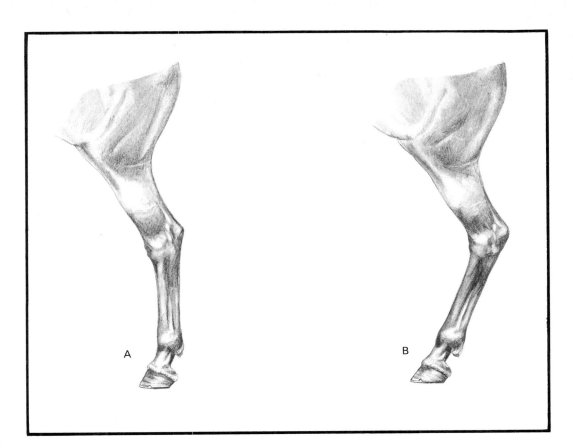

Left: Good and bad hind legs
a) Normal hind leg
b) Sickle hock

Below: Trotting across a field. Turning horses free is an excellent way of judging their action. This Lipizzaner is showing a good, long stride at the trot. (*Sylvester Jacobs*)

Right: The action of the
horse at the gallop. One of
the earliest series of
photographs taken which
illustrated the sequence of
footfalls, and disproved
previous theories. (*BBC
Hulton Picture Library*)

foreleg and right hind leg then do the same after which for a moment
the horse is suspended in the air without a foot touching the ground.
As he achieves this moment of suspension he thrusts the rider upwards.
The experienced horseman has supple hips and back which enable him
to absorb this movement and remain in the saddle. The alternative is
to post-rise to the trot: the rider puts his weight in the stirrups and
comes out of the saddle for this moment and return as the horse's legs
hit the ground.

At the canter (known as the lope by Western riders) three hoof beats
are heard. The horse can either lead with the right or left leg; on the
right lead the right front foot strikes the ground in advance of the left,
and on the left lead the left front foot strikes in advance of the right. On
both leads there is a moment of suspension when all four legs are in the
air. As the canter gets faster and the strides are extended then this
moment of suspension becomes longer and four hoof beats are heard – it
is then known as the gallop.

When looking at the action of a horse it is important that his gaits
are true, i.e. that the correct number of hoof beats are heard. It is not
uncommon for the walk to become two-time and the canter four-time.
These are not serious faults for the general riding horse, but would be
for a show or dressage horse.

The next important factor in a horse's action is that active steps are
taken. Horses that drag one or more of their limbs along the ground
have either some weakness or are not athletic. Excessive wear on the
front of the shoe is a good indication of this fault. It is particularily
important that this activity applies to the hind legs so that they step
well under the body. It is only when they do this that the horse can
develop that vital power of propulsion.

Another important aspect of the horse's action is that it is relatively

straight. If the pairs of fore or hind legs come too close together they can brush and cause damage. In addition any swings or twists usually lead to undue strain on one or more of the joints. When viewed head on at the walk and trot the forelegs should sweep straight forward; if they turn too far out the horse is said to 'dish', and if they turn inward the horse is accused of being 'pigeon toed'.

Soundness

So far we have discussed the best shape and movement in horses to enable them to carry out their work. A beautiful horse with magnificent movement is of no value, however, if he is unsound. Obvious unsoundness can usually be detected by any experienced horseman but internal or potential problems are usually only exposed after a veterinary examination; sometimes even X-rays are needed. The following are some of the most common reasons for unsoundness in horses.

Respiratory defects are often found in horses but are more prevalent in older and/or larger animals. Possible causes are weaknesses in conformation or from being worked too soon after or even during a heavy cold or virus. Probably the most serious defect is broken wind which results in a persistent cough and an exaggerated double heaving of the flanks during exhalation. This is a result of the breakdown of the air vesicles or vessels of the lungs and is with few exceptions incurable. The effects can be alleviated by keeping the victim away from dust.

A whistler is a horse which makes a whistling noise when inhaling due to the paralysis of a vocal chord. Operations (e.g. hobdaying) usually cure this. Roaring on the other hand – when the horse makes a rumbling noise when exhaling – is difficult to cure. It is caused by paralysis of the soft palate and although operable is rarely improved.

Right: Another early series of Muybridge photographs which illustrated the action of the horse when cantering over an obstacle. (*BBC Hulton Picture Library*)

These three defects restrict a horse's breathing. Long and fast work is difficult and in more serious cases even less arduous activity is a strain. This type of unsoundness, however, rarely renders a horse useless. Riders attracted by the cheaper price of an unsound animal can confine them to less strenuous activities. Nor should wind problems be confused with high blowing, when a horse makes a noise upon exhaling. This is due to an abnormality in the false nostril and it does not restrict the breathing.

Lameness or weakness which is likely to produce lameness in the future are more usual reasons for a horse being considered unsound. If the lameness is due to such problems as a wound, injury, prick or puncture of the foot, corns (bruises to the sole in the heel region of the foot), sand crack (vertical crack in the hoof), then it can probably be cured and there is little need to worry about the horse's future value for work.

There are also some deformities which rarely cause lameness and only in exceptionally bad cases constitute an unsoundness. These include a bog spavin (soft round swelling on the front inner side of the hock), thoroughpin (soft swelling above and in front of the point of the hock), wind galls (soft round swellings just above the fetlock), and curb (a hard enlargement below the point of the hock). Some veterinary surgeons consider the latter an unsoundness but although it is an eyesore I have never heard of it causing lameness.

Then there are splints – bony enlargements which are usually found on the inside of the fore legs. These can cause lameness as they form, but if the animal is rested the pain rarely lasts longer than six weeks.

Strained tendons are another cause of lameness; they can be cured,

Above: Many horses, especially Thoroughbreds, are bought and sold at auctions. This is one of the most famous 'rings' – Tattersalls, Newmarket, England. (*Sally Anne Thompson*)

but less easily than splints. The tendons liable to strain are those between the knee and the fetlock on the front leg and they are particularly susceptible to strain in horses which have to gallop when tired – racehorses and eventers. If a horse is to be used for these sports then it is dangerous to choose one with a history of tendon problems or indications of heat or puffiness in this area. On the other hand, if the problem is not too serious and/or if the tendons have been treated successfully by firing, split tendon operation or carbon fibre insertions, then the horse should be able to stand up to less arduous work.

There are some causes of lameness which are incurable and a horse which shows signs of them is likely to become an invalid sooner or later. These include pedal ostitis (bruising of the pedal bone in the foot), navicular (the navicular bone in the foot acquires a different shape and texture which makes it a painful surface for the flexor tendon to run over), bone spavin (a hard, bony enlargement on the lower and inner side of the hock), and ring bone (a bony enlargement of the pastern bone). The last may not be as serious as the others and may not cause lameness until the horse is old.

Numerous defects have been listed in this chapter and no horse will be without a few of them – the perfect horse does not exist. For the potential purchaser or anyone interested in assessing a horse the important thing to do is to weigh up the effect any defects will have on the work proposed for the horse, and also to see if the defect can be balanced by a particularly good quality elsewhere – e.g. a weak second thigh but powerful hindquarters. Those who love horses find this examination of the horse's make, shape and action and the challenge of judging its potential a fascinating occupation.

The Popular Breeds of Horse

'Breed' in the horse world has a number of different definitions. In this book it is taken to mean a well-defined type of horse for which there is a breed society promoting its production and controlling a stud book. Many of the breeds do not breed true to type; even the Thoroughbred comes in all shapes and sizes. In addition some of the stud books are still open, which means that parents of different breeds are accepted. A Hanoverian, for example, might have a Hanoverian mother and a Thoroughbred father, for this breed society accepts outcrossing with certain recognized breeds.

In order to identify the popular breeds of the world they have been divided into categories: Ponies – horses under 14.2hh; Hotbloods – spirited horses like the Arabs and their descendants, the Thoroughbreds; Coldbloods – heavywork horses thought to be descendants of the prehistoric Forest rather than the Plains horse; and Warmbloods – riding and driving horses which are a mixture of Coldbloods, Hotbloods and Ponies.

Hotbloods

Arab is the oldest pure bred in the world. Its original colours were bay or chestnut but today grey is quite common. It has a small tapering head and concave profile, large dark eyes, small alert ears set wide apart, an arched neck, a long sloping shoulder, a short straight back, a straight croup and the tail is set high. The legs are fine but the bone is exceptionally hard. It is fast, has great powers of endurance, and its action is free and floating. It is used for a multitude of purposes including general riding, long distance racing and being used to improve other breeds.

The desert Arab was thought to have originated in the Yemen and stood about 14.3hh. The Persian Arab is a slightly larger version: it is the oldest known domesticated horse and is claimed to be the forerunner of the Arab breed. Egypt has also bred the Arab for centuries and has some of the best specimens in the world. The other country claiming a high quality Arabian is Poland.

The Arab has become an international breed with practically every country organizing its own stud book for the breed. Some of the best specimens of the breed are no longer found in their original habitat but have been exported to Germany, France, USA, Australia and the UK.

Thoroughbred is another international breed. It was developed in Britain between the seventeenth and nineteenth centuries from Oriental imports and in particular three stallions – Byerley Turk, Darley Arabian and Godolphin Arabian. Today it is the fastest horse in the world, stands between 15.1hh and 17hh and varies in shape from close-coupled

sprinters with large powerful hindquarters to big-framed, big-boned steeplechasers. Most have an elegant head, a long neck, sloping shoulder, prominent wither, and a silky coat. They have spirited temperaments and although bred for the racecourse are used for every type of riding and for the refining of heavier breeds of horses.

Above: The Arab is found around the world, and local varieties have been developed such as this Shagya Arab which is bred in Hungary. (*Sally Anne Thompson*)

Warmbloods

Akhal Teke is one of Russia's most famous breeds. Of Turkoman stock, it stands about 15hh and although coming in most whole colours usually has a metallic bloom to its coat. It is an elegant horse with a long body and legs. It is hardy, spirited and fast and is used for riding and competitions.

Albino is treated as a breed in the USA but elsewhere these horses which are white with pink skin and have pale blue or dark brown eyes are occasional freaks. In the USA they are used as riding horses and were originally produced from Arab and Morgan stock.

Alter Real is bred in Portugal. It stands about 15.2hh and is usually chestnut, bay or piebald. It is an elegant, spirited horse, close coupled with powerful hindquarters. It has extravagant high knee action and this, together with its intelligence has made it popular for High School work. It is an offshoot of the neighbouring Andalusian breed to which Arab, Thoroughbred, Norman and Hanoverian blood has been added.

49

The Popular Breeds of Horse

Right: A Thoroughbred mare and foal at Spendthrift, which is one of the most famous and luxurious of the American racehorse studs. (*Sally Anne Thompson*)

Below, left: The Akhal Teke, characterized by the golden sheen to its coat. This mare and foal are roaming the grasslands of the Tersk stud. (*Sally Anne Thompson*)

Below, right: The Alter Real, a Portuguese breed renowned for its spectacular action which makes it a good High School horse. (*Sally Anne Thompson*)

Andalusian has been bred in Spain since the Middle Ages. It stands about 15.3hh, is usually grey and has a large, almost convex profile to its head. The neck is strong and arched, the body short and the hindquarters powerful. Its intelligence, athletic ability, great presence and elegant springy action has made it one of the most popular High School horses. Its foundation stock is thought to be Garrano and Noriker ponies mixed with the Arabs and Barbs brought in by the Oriental invaders.

Appaloosa is an American breed of Spanish origins. It stands about 15hh and has one of six basic patterns of spots on either a grey or roan base. There is a characteristic white sclera around the eye and it has a thin mane and tail. Originally bred by the Indians, it is now used as a circus horse or a cow pony, and as a pleasure and parade horse.

Australian Stock Horse was only recently given a stud book in Australia. It stands around 15.3hh and comes in a variety of colours and shapes. It is renowned for its stamina, hardiness and maneouvrability. It is used for herding stock and in rodeos, and was originally developed largely from Thoroughbred, Arab and Spanish stock.

Barb bred in Algeria and Morocco is similar to the Arab but has a longer head with a straight profile. The hindquarters are more sloping and the tail lower set. It is frugal, tough and is thought to have developed from European, rather than the Asian Wild Stock that was the foundation of the Arab. It is used for riding and transport.

Bavarian is one of the ten regional breeds of riding horses in West Germany. It is a thick-set riding horse which originated from the battle charger of the region – the Rottaler. More recently Thoroughbred, Cleveland Bay and Norman blood has been used for refining the breed.

Budenny bred in Russia from Thoroughbred, Don and Kazakh stock stands about 15.3hh and is chestnut or bay with a golden sheen. It is a strong elegant horse which is fast and has stamina. It is used for riding, competitions and steeplechasing.

Calabrese is bred in Italy, coming originally from the famous but now extinct High School horses – the Neapolitans. It stands about 16hh and is a middleweight riding horse.

Cleveland Bay is a multi-purpose British breed. Developed by the Yorkshire farmers from their native Chapman horses and Thoroughbreds, it is always bay or brown. It is a strong horse with a longish back and a high-set tail. It is used in harness, for light agricultural work and for general riding.

Criollo is the tough pony which developed wild on the Argentinian pampas from the Arabs, Barbs and Andalusians which got free from the original settlers. It stands about 14.2hh and is usually dun with dark points, red or blue roan, sorrel or skewbald. It has a short-coupled, sturdy frame with short legs and good bone. It is very tough, manoeuvrable and willing, and is used for long-distance riding and ranch work.

Crioulo is Brazil's version of the Criollo. It is usually lighter in colour and has prominent withers, a high set tail and a longish neck. Alter Real stock from Portugal mixed with Criollos was its foundation stock.

Danish Sportshorse was developed in the last two decades by the Danes to meet the demands for riding horses. Hanoverian, Anglo-Norman, Swedish-Warmblood, Trakehner, Polish and native halfbred blood was used. It comes in a variety of colours and sizes and is renowned for its sensible temperament, good action and athletic ability.

Danubian is Bulgaria's riding horse developed from Anglo-Arab and Nonius blood. It is usually black or dark chestnut, is short coupled, has a deep girth and high-set tail. It is strong and used for light draught work as well as riding and competitions. It stands about 15.2hh.

Døle is bred in Norway and is dark in colour. There is a larger version, about 15.1hh which is used for draught work and in harness; and a smaller pony type which has an upright shoulder, round hindquarters, short legs and little feather. Both were developed from Danish Coldbloods, Thoroughbreds and Trotters. Recently more trotter stock has been added to some of these Døles to develop the Døle Trotter which is used for the very popular trotting races.

Don is the Cossack horse from the USSR. It originated largely from Oriental, Thoroughbred and Orlov stock but in the nineteenth century Turkoman, Karabakh and Karabair blood was added. It usually stands about 15.2hh and is coloured chestnut, bay or grey. It has a long straight neck and back, is long in the leg and has great stamina. Today it is used for harness work, general riding and long-distance racing.

East Bulgarian is Bulgaria's lighter riding horse. It stands about 15.3hh and is usually chestnut or black. It has a smallish head with a straight profile, a deep girth and a long straight back. It is a lively, versatile horse which is used in everything from agriculture to steeple-chasing. It was developed from Anglo-Arab, Arab, Thoroughbred and local halfbred horses.

East Friesian is an East German breed which is a refined version of the Oldenburg, from which it is derived, with the addition of Arab and Hanoverian stock. It stands about 16.1hh and is used for riding and light draught work.

Franches Montagnes, also known as Freiberger, is Switzerland's work horse. Standing about 15.1hh, it is found in most colours. It has a powerful compact frame with stamina and strength and is used in agriculture and transport. It was developed by crossing the Freiberger coldblood with the Shagya Arab.

Fredericksborg was once Denmark's most popular breed, but is now quite rare. It was developed from Andalusian and Neapolitan stock. It is usually chestnut, stands 15.3hh and is a strong plain harness horse with a big chest. It has a good temperament and is used for light draught work and general riding.

Below: A Hackney dating back to their 'golden era' at the end of the last century. At that time they were used in large numbers for showing and for pulling elegant carriages. (*British Library*)

Below: An Appaloosa foal. This eye-catching American breed was originally developed by the Nez Percé Indians who believed the spots were useful camouflage. (*Sally Anne Thompson*)

Right: The Cleveland Bay, originally a dual-purpose carriage and farm horse, is today often crossed with Thoroughbreds to produce animals like this. (*Sylvester Jacobs*)

French Anglo-Arab breeds pretty true to type and is not merely the result of crossing Thoroughbreds and Arabs as in other countries. It has been developed over the last two centuries from Oriental stock in south-west France, as well as Arabs and Thoroughbreds. It stands about 16hh and is a well-proportioned, powerful horse with stamina and good movement. It is used for general riding, competitions and racing.

French Trotter was developed by the French in the last century largely from Thoroughbred, Norfolk Trotter and Norman blood. It stands about 16.1hh and is a tall, light-framed horse, with a strong back and sloping hindquarters. It is athletic and fast, and although used largely for harness racing, is also used in general riding and for cross-breeding.

Friesian is an old Dutch breed of black horse. It stands about 15hh and has a longish head, crested neck, good bone, feather and a full mane and tail. It has a docile, sensitive temperament and is used in harness, for circus work and general riding.

Furioso was produced from British halfbreds imported into Hungary in the nineteenth century. It is a robust horse standing over 15.3hh and is used for riding, competitions and steeplechasing.

Gelderland is Holland's famous carriage horse. Standing about 15.2hh it is usually chestnut or grey, short coupled, has extravagant action and great 'presence'.

Hackney is a more refined version (Thoroughbred blood having been added), of Britain's famous but now extinct Norfolk Trotter. It stands about 15.1hh, comes in dark colours and has a spectacular high-stepping action. Its smaller relative, the Hackney Pony, was the result of crosses with the Fell and Dale.

Hanoverian is West Germany's most successful competition horse. It can be traced back to the Great War Horse, and has been refined largely by Arab, Thoroughbred and Cleveland Bay blood. It is a large powerful horse, famous for its extravagant action and great athletic ability.

Holstein, also bred in Germany, has a heavier frame than the Hanoverian. It is usually black, bay or brown and has good action. It is used for riding and harness work. It can be traced back to the Marsh Horse and was refined with Oriental and Andalusian stock and later Thoroughbred and Cleveland.

Iomud is another Russian horse to come from Turkoman stock. It is similar but more compact than the Akhal Teke. It is used for distance racing, general riding and for the cavalry.

Karabair is one of the many breeds in the USSR to have Mongolian and Arab ancestors. It is an ancient mountain breed which looks similar to the Arab and is used for riding and local sports, and for agricultural work.

Page 54, below, left: The Danish Sportshorse has had its stud book for little more than a decade, but is fast establishing a reputation as an athletic horse, as shown by this bucking member of the breed. (*Sylvester Jacobs*)

Pages 54/55, below, right: A Friesian, an eye-catching breed of black horse which has been bred for centuries in Holland. (*W. Slob, Robert Harding Associates*)

Right: The Nonius, a Hungarian breed of riding horse which is bred in large quantities at the country's state studs. (*Sally Anne Thompson*)

Below, left: A Hanoverian when only a few months old. Its legs are too long and the neck too short as yet for it to reach the grass in a normal fashion. (*Jane Kidd*)

Karabakh was developed in the USSR hundreds of years ago from Persian, Turkoman and Arab blood. It is usually dun, bay or chestnut with a metallic sheen. A tough mountain horse, it is now used for riding, equestrian games and racing.

Karacabey is being bred in Turkey from crosses between native mares and Nonius. It is used for riding, light draught, agriculture, cavalry and pack work.

Knabstrup is a Danish spotted horse which was derived from the Fredericksborg and is now used mainly in the circus.

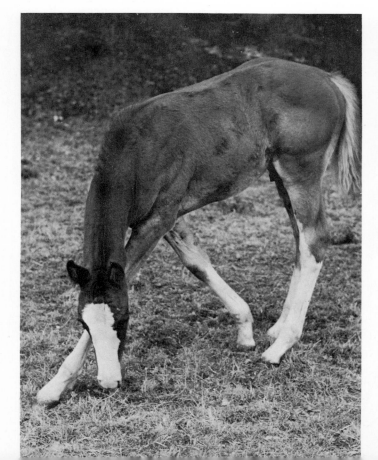

Kladrub is Czechoslovakia's grey horse, famous for carriage work. A heavier version of the Andalusian, it was derived from crosses between this breed and the Oldenburg, Hanoverian and Anglo-Norman.

Lipizzaner is thought of as an Austrian horse although its original home, the stud of Lipizza, lies in Czechoslovakia. This intelligent, compact, athletic grey horse is the most famous High School horse in the world. It originated in Spain, hence the name of Spanish Riding School for its place of work.

Lusitano is an ancient Portuguese breed with few modern representatives. Originating from Andalusian and Arab blood, it is a tough, short-coupled horse used in the bullring and by the cavalry.

Mecklenburg is the East German version of the Hanoverian but is a little smaller.

Morgan is one of America's most versatile horses. Standing about 15hh, it is usually dark in colour with a stocky, powerful frame. It has high action and is used for numerous activities both under saddle and in harness. Its ancestors were of Welsh Cob and Thoroughbred origins.

Mustang still runs wild in the USA. It is little more than a pony and comes in all sizes and colours, but is particularly sturdy and tough. When broken, it is used for every type of riding.

Below: The Karabair, which is a Russian breed. It is a heavier version of the Arab which has been bred and used in mountainous areas for centuries. (*Sally Anne Thompson*)

Nonius was developed as a riding horse in Hungary from stock from most European countries. It varies a good deal in height but is generally over 15hh. It is versatile, long lived, and used for riding and agriculture.

Novokirghiz is a new Russian breed established by refining the Kirghiz with Don and Thoroughbred blood. It stands about 15hh, has a long body, is tough and sure-footed, which makes it suitable for mountain work, and also provides milk.

Oldenburg is the largest and heaviest of the German riding horses. It stands about 16.3hh and matures early; it has a docile temperament and is most famous as a carriage horse.

Orlov is a handsome largish grey, bay or black horse used for harness racing. Count Orlov developed the breed in the USSR from a mixture of European breeds but the foundation stock was an Arab and Dutch or Danish mare.

Palomino has a stud book in the USA but does not breed true to type. All registered stock are golden with no markings other than white on the face or below the knees. The mane and tail are white, silver or ivory and the eyes are dark.

Paso Fino is a smallish horse developed from Spanish stock in Puerto Rico. It is a strong, spirited horse and has unusual gaits, the slowest of which is known as the paso fino, then the paso cort and the fastest the paso largo.

Peruvian Stepping Horse developed from Spanish and Andalusian stock. It is usually bay or chestnut, about 15hh, strong, and has a special gait (of about 11mph/18km) which is similar to an amble and is comfortable for long journeys.

Pinto is another American horse which varies in type but has an unusual colour, in this case black with white or white with any colour but black. It is used for ranch work, the show ring and general riding.

Quarter Horse is America's most popular horse. Originally bred from Arab, Barb, Turkish, Thoroughbred and Andalusian horses, all stock was tested over a quarter of a mile – hence the name. Chestnut is the most common colour. It has a short head, powerful short body, large round hindquarters and fine legs. It is exceptionally fast over short distances and very manoeuvrable. It is used for racing, ranch work, rodeos and the show ring.

Russian Trotter is the result of crossing Orlovs with Standardbreds in order to produce a faster horse for racing. There are more than thirty state studs breeding trotting horses in Russia.

Saddlebred is America's unique riding horse. Its most important ancestors were the now extinct Narragansett Pacer and the Thoroughbred. It stands about 15.2hh, comes in solid colours, has a small head, crested neck, strong body and hindquarters, and a full mane and tail. It also has a high tail carriage produced by nicking the muscles in the dock and carrying it in a crupper. Five-gaited saddlebreds, as the name implies, can perform five gaits. In addition to the walk, trot and canter there is the rack – a very fast four-beat gait, when all four feet are in the air simultaneously and then come down separately, and a slower version known as the slow gait. They are used in the show ring, for riding and harness work.

Selle Français is France's riding horse. It was established in the 1960s with the amalgamation of all French regional breeds of riding horse (Anglo-Norman, Vendeen, Limousin etc.). Its shape, size and colour varies but it has a good temperament, is athletic and is used for general riding and competitions.

Standardbred is used in America's harness races. Standing about 15.2hh, it is a muscular Thoroughbred type but has a longer back, shorter legs and powerful shoulder. It has a variety of ancestors which includes the Hackney, Thoroughbred, Narragansett Pacer, Barb and Canadian Trotter.

Swedish Halfbred developed as a cavalry remount and has had a stud book for a hundred years. It comes in a variety of sizes and colours but most have smallish heads, large bold eyes, extravagant action and are athletic. They have proved to be excellent competition horses. For the last hundred years a good deal of Trakehner, Hanoverian and Thoroughbred blood has been added.

Tennessee Walker is one of America's most spectacular breeds. Usually about 15.2hh, with its powerful body and full mane and tail it is a wonderful sight in its unique running walk when the forefeet are raised high. It was developed from other American breeds such as the Narragansett Pacer, Standardbred, Morgan and Saddlebred in the last century.

Trakehner was the most famous German breed until its stock was split between East and West as a result of World War II. It stands about 16.1hh, is elegant with a head that is broad between the eyes and tapers to the muzzle, the neck is long and the hindquarters flat. It is used for riding and competitions.

Turkoman is derived from the horses left by the raiding Mongols and the horses bred by the Scythians in 100AD and is still bred in Iran today. It has a narrow, light frame, but is fast and tough. It is used as the foundation stock for many other breeds and is a cavalry, riding and race horse.

Right: A Palomino – a colour of horse found all over the world, but in the US they are so popular and numerous that they have their own stud book. (*Sally Anne Thompson*)

Below: The Quarter Horse. This stocky powerful breed was developed in the US; but many, including this example, have been exported to Australia. (*Country Life, Australia*)

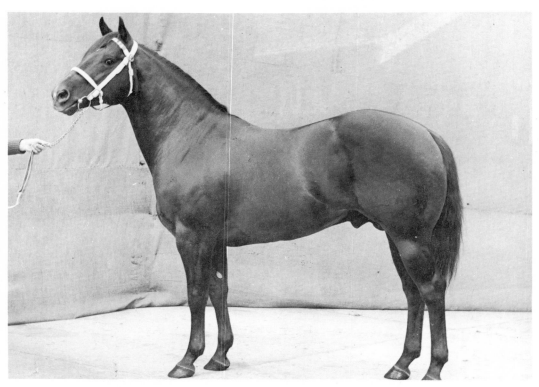

Welsh Cob is one of Britain's most versatile and eye-catching breeds. Ranging from about 14 to 15.1hh, these compact horses have great substance, quality and silky feather on their legs. They were derived from Trotter, Oriental and Welsh Pony stock. They have a high knee action and are equally at home under rider or in harness.

Wielkopolsi is a Polish breed formed by the amalgamation of the Masuren and Poznan. It is a compact, well-proportioned horse which is used for riding, competitions and light draught. Its ancestors are the Trakehner, Konik and Thoroughbred.

Ponies

Asiatic Wild Horse, also known as Mongolian Wild Horse and Equus Przewalskii is the last of the wild horses. Standing 13.1hh, it is dun with a dorsal stripe, dark points and the primitive features of a big head, upright mane, thin tail and upright shoulder.

Avelignese is the Italian version of Austria's Haflinger.

Balearic is a pony of ancient origins found on Majorca. It is dark in colour, has a fine head with a Roman nose and a light, tough frame. It is used in agriculture and in harness.

Bali is one of the Indonesian ponies derived from Asiatic Wild stock. It stands about 12.2hh and is dun with a dorsal stripe and dark points.

Bashkirsky is a bay, dun or chestnut pony found in the USSR. It is thickset with a longish back and is used for riding and pulling sleighs. The mares are milked for 'kumiss', a medicinal and alcoholic drink.

Basque is a French pony which still roams wild in the Pyrenees and Atlantic cantons. It stands about 13hh and has a primitive appearance.

Basuto is South Africa's only breed. It stands about 14.2hh, has a quality head and a long neck and back. It is sure-footed and tough, and is used for racing, polo and general riding. It was derived from imported Arab, Barb and Thoroughbred stock.

Batak is one of the best Indonesian ponies, in which a strong infusion of Arab blood has left its mark. It stands about 12.2hh, varies in shape and colour and is used for agriculture and transportation.

Bosnian, standing little more than 12.2hh, is in great demand in Yugoslavia on the farms and for pack work. It is a compact mountain pony which has a mixture of Tarpan and Eastern blood.

Camargue is the famous wild grey pony from France's marshlands on the Rhone delta. It has an oriental head probably derived from its alleged ancestor, the Barb, with a long straight shoulder and a short body. When caught it is used as a mount for the Camargue cowboys or *gardiens*, for herding bulls and trekking by tourists.

Connemara has been bred on the west coast of Eire for centuries. It is thought to have had some Arab and Spanish stock added after the sinking of the Spanish Armada. It is usually grey, has an intelligent head and a sturdy body. It is used for riding and harness work.

Dale is one of the largest and strongest of Britain's mountain and moorland breeds. It is dark in colour and is used for pack, agricultural work and riding. It is a slightly larger version of its neighbour the Fell and the two have many ancestors in common. These are thought to include Britain's old racing pony the Galloway, Welsh Cob, Friesian and Celtic.

Dartmoor is bred in the south of England on the moors after which it was named. It is usually dark in colour, stands about 12.1hh and is used mainly for riding.

Exmoor is the Dartmoor's neighbour to the south. The oldest of the British breeds, it stands 12hh and is usually bay, brown or dun with black points and a light, mealy muzzle.

Falabella was developed in the Argentine from Shetland and Thoroughbred stock. Standing just 7hh it is used as a harness pony and a pet.

Fell is usually a little smaller version of the Dale but is similar in its colour and great strength.

Fjord is a very old breed tracing back to the Asiatic Wild Horse. Its original home was Norway but this dun pony with its dark dorsal stripe and upright black and silver mane is now found all over Europe. It stands about 14hh and its strength and stamina make it popular as a work pony, in harness and for riding.

Galiceño, found in Mexico, traces back to the Garrano which was brought over by the European invaders. It is usually bay, black, sorrel or dun, is short-coupled, narrow in its body frame and has a natural running walk. It is used on the ranches as well as for general riding.

Garrano is a Portuguese breed. Standing just 11hh, it is dark chestnut with a light frame and a full mane and tail.

Gotland is a very old breed which has inhabited the Swedish island, after which it was named, for centuries. Its ancestors were Tarpans but its lighter frame is probably due to infusions of oriental blood in the nineteenth century.

Haflinger, Austria's most famous pony, is an old breed with Arab influences. The colour is eye-catching – chestnut with flaxen mane and tail. It has an elegant head but more common hindquarters. It has long been used as a mountain pony and is popular today in harness.

Huçul is also known as the Carpathian Pony. It originated from a mixture of Tarpan and Arab stock. Its home is Poland where this dun or bay pony is used in the mountains by farmers and transporters.

Java is another of Indonesia's work ponies and is best known for pulling 'sados', which are two-wheeled taxis. It is a strong pony standing about 12.2hh.

Kathiawari from India stands about 14.2hh and is a light, narrow pony used for pack, transport and riding. It is the result of mixing Arab blood with the indigenous Indian pony.

Kazakh is a Russian pony which stands 13hh and is similar to its ancestor the Mongolian Wild Horse. It is used for riding and herding; meat and milk are taken from the mares.

Konik is a Polish pony which stands 13.1hh and is descended from the Tarpan. It is usually yellow, grey or blue dun with a dorsal stripe and is used by the lowland farmers.

Manipuri is a thickset pony from India and was the original polo pony. It is little more than 12hh and is a mixture of Asiatic Wild Horse stock and Arab.

New Forest is the least uniform of Britain's mountain and moorland ponies because it has interbred with many other ponies which were set free in its original home, the New Forest. It is usually dark in colour, very tough and adaptable in order to survive often severe weather conditions and is used for riding.

Above: A Fjord, a very old Norwegian breed distinguished by its upright mane and a dorsal stripe which runs from the ears to the tail. (*E. Preston*)

Pindos is a small Greek pony with ancient origins. It is very tough and used for riding and light agricultural work; the mares are used for breeding mules.

Shetland is the smallest of the British ponies, the tiniest standing 6.2hh. It is black or brown, with a small head, a very full mane and tail, and has a thick coat in winter and sleek one in summer. It is very strong for its size and is used for riding and driving. Its origins are similar to those of the Exmoor.

Sorraia is a Portuguese pony of Tarpan origins. It stands about 13hh, and is dun with a dorsal stripe. It is primitive in appearance and runs wild.

Sumba is an Indonesian pony with Mongolian origins. It is another primitive type and is dun with a dorsal stripe. Apart from general work it is used as a dancing pony.

Tarpan is a modern version of the Ice Age horse. Today it either runs wild in the forests of Poland or is kept in zoos. It stands about 13hh, is brown or mouse dun with a dorsal stripe, and has a dark mane and tail. It has a long head, long ears, a short neck and a long back with fine legs.

Viatka is a Russian descendant of the Klepper and Konik. It stands about 13.2hh, is dark and sometimes has a dorsal stripe. It is a sturdy, tough and fast all-purpose pony.

Welsh is the most elegant of Britain's ponies. There are divisions according to size and the oldest and smallest (less than 12hh) is the Welsh Mountain Pony. Oriental and Andalusian influences are apparent in its eye-catching conformation and spirited and intelligent character. The Welsh Ponies are larger, as a result of crosses between the Welsh Mountain and Cob, and are used for riding and harness work. They are also popular as children's riding and show ponies.

Zemaituka is a Russian descendant of the Asiatic Wild Horse and the Arab. It stands about 13.2hh, and is brown, palomino or dun with a dorsal stripe.

Coldbloods

Ardennais, like the mountains where they live, are divided into French and Belgian Ardennais. The Swedes also took the breed to their country and developed the Swedish Ardennes. It usually stands about 15.3hh, is bay, chestnut or roan with a muscular short-coupled body. It is used in agriculture and in Sweden for timber hauling.

Boulonnais is one of France's most elegant heavy horses. It has similar origins to the Percheron, is usually grey, chestnut or bay and stands about 16.1hh. Quite numerous at one time, the numbers were considerably reduced by losses in the two world wars.

Brabant, also known as the Belgian after its country of origin, is a descendant of the Flanders Horse, the famous mount of the knights of the Middle Ages. It is red, roan with black points or chestnut, has a heavy large frame, a short back and short legs with feather on the fetlocks.

Breton is a smaller French heavy horse standing about 15.2hh. The smaller, more elegant version is known as the Postier and the larger, stronger one as the Draught.

Clydesdale is Scotland's heavy horse. It stands about 16.2hh, is bay or brown with white on the face and legs. It is an especially active heavy horse and very popular because of the ease with which it copes with heavy work.

Finnish stands about 15.2hh. It is chestnut, bay or brown. Apart from hauling the timber for which its country is famous, it is fast enough for trotting races.

Irish Draught is light and agile enough to go hunting, the favourite sport of so many Irish farmers. It stands about 16hh, is bay, brown or grey, has good bone, a little feather, large round feet and strong sloping hindquarters. Today it is used mainly for crossing with Thoroughbreds to breed riding horses.

Jutland was named after this agricultural area of Denmark where it was developed from native stock, Suffolk Punches, Yorkshire Coach Horses and the Cleveland Bay. It stands about 15.3hh, is usually chestnut or roan and is a massive, compact horse.

Lithuanian was developed in Russia by crossing their native Zemaituka with imported heavy horses from Scandinavia. It is usually bay, black or chestnut with flaxen mane and tail, stands about 15.3hh and has a kind temperament.

Muraköz is an eye-catching Hungarian heavy horse. It is chestnut with a flaxen mane and tail, and has a strong frame and rounded hindquarters. It has been developed this century by crossing native mares with Oriental, Percheron and Ardennais stock.

Noriker was developed in the Roman province of Noricum which today falls between Austria and Bavaria. Also known as the South German Coldblood, it is chestnut, bay or spotted. It is strong and sure-footed which makes it one of the best heavy horses for mountain work.

Percheron is France's beautiful heavy horse. Usually grey or black, it has an Oriental-type head, a strong, well-proportioned body, full mane and tail, clean hard legs with no feather and moves actively and well with a light gait. It is a descendant of Oriental, Norman and native heavy stock.

Rhenish German is similar to the Belgian from which it was developed in Germany in the last century.

Russian Heavy Draught, standing about 14.2hh, is one of the smallest of the Coldbloods. It is chestnut, bay or roan, thick-set, strong and active. It was developed by crossing imported heavy horses with the Orlov and indigenous Ukraine breeds.

Schleswig Heavy Draught was developed in the last century in Germany from a good deal of imported stock – Jutlands, Bretons, Boulonnais and Suffolk Punches. It is chestnut with a flaxen mane and tail, and is similar to the Jutland.

Shire is the tallest and strongest of the heavy horses: it stands about 17hh. It is alleged to be a descendant of the horses William the Conqueror brought to England, and was developed as a breed for draught work in the British Midlands. It is bay or brown with white markings, particularly powerful hindquarters and plenty of silky feather on its legs.

Suffolk Punch was developed in the east of England into a very uniform type, all standing about 16.1hh. They are chestnut with no white markings, no feather on the legs, massive short bodies and good action.

Vladimir Heavy Draught is another heavy horse from the USSR which was developed from imported stock. It stands about 16hh, has a strong frame, good conformation and feather on the legs.

Right: The Suffolk Punch, one of the most placid and strongest of the heavy horses. It is bred in East Anglia in the UK. (*Sally Anne Thompson*)

Below: The Clydesdale in a frisky mood. This British breed of heavy horse was developed for work in transport and agriculture, but gradually over this century has been superseded by the tractor and lorry. (*Sally Anne Thompson*)

The Horse in History

The animal of war

For more than 3500 years the horse was a decisive instrument of war. Their era started about 1750BC when the Aryans, who had lived in the mountain ranges around the Black and Caspian Seas, migrated southwards into Mesopotamia. They were all-conquering because they had the monopoly of an invincible weapon of war – the horse-drawn chariot. It ended in 1939 when the Poles mounted a series of futile cavalry charges against the might of the German Army and were heavily defeated. This tragedy in Poland gave dramatic emphasis to the end of the horse as an important influence in man's struggle for power.

The Aryans used the mobility of the chariot to devastating effect against infantry, but the opposition quickly corrected this handicap by building their own chariots, and this new method of warfare spread around the civilized world: first to Egypt, then to Greece and India.

Chariots became increasingly sophisticated with up to three or four ponies in harness. They were used in war for many centuries. In 55BC the British were still using them as a vital part of their defence against Julius Caesar's invading army.

The horses that first drew the chariots are thought to have been quite small, but with food and selective breeding they became larger, until they became big enough to carry men. They were now a more effective weapon of war than the cumbersome chariot. Warriors discovered that when they were mounted on fleet-footed horses they were not such easy targets and were able to withdraw quickly when necessary.

The first cavalry is thought to have been formed by the Assyrians. There is a reference to the cavalry of the victorious Assyrian Army in a battle against the King of Nairi in 890BC, although cavalry probably existed some time before this. However, horsemen must have had a pretty hair-raising time, for the tactics were to charge, let go the reins in order to shoot off arrows from their bows, then wheel around and gallop back out of range – all without saddles.

Military supremacy passed from the Assyrians to the Persians, who rode larger and stronger horses, in the sixth century BC. They, like the Greeks who were to follow them as the major military power, rode their horses with more collection and control than the Assyrians who charged at extended paces, and with their reins loose.

The Greeks have left us some beautiful art and some fascinating literature about the use of the horse in war. Alexander The Great is one of their greatest heroes with his feats of horsemanship and brilliant use of his cavalry. It was his outstanding handling of the cavalry, a force built up by his father, Philip of Macedon, which enabled him to conquer such a large area of the world from 330BC to 320BC. His charger in most of his campaigns until he was killed at the Battle of

Above: Chariots were used for sport as well as war. Chariot races were the first equestrian sport included at the Olympic Games. This is a victor parading in Ancient Rome. (*Peter Newark's Historical Pictures*)

Left: Attila, leader of the Huns who were thought to be the first horsemen to use stirrups. These helped them in their conquests of much of the Roman Empire during the fifth century AD. (*Peter Newark's Historical Pictures*)

69

Hudaspes against the Indian, King Porus, was the celebrated Bucephalus.

The story of how Alexander acquired Bucephalus has been embellished through the ages, but there must be some truth in it. Alexander was said to be just twelve years old when this magnificent horse, for which Philip had paid a vast price, was brought to the Macedonian Court. Bucephalus quickly discharged all the men who attempted to ride him, but Alexander begged to try. His father scoffed, but his son simply turned the head of the horse towards the sun, mounted him and trotted away through the crowd. Bucephalus had been frightened of his shadow. Alexander was perceptive enough to notice this and had the courage to try out his theory – these were characteristics which won him many battles.

The Romans were more famous for their use of infantry rather than cavalry, but one of their defeats was due to a lack of horsepower. Caesar's first attempt to conquer Britain in 55BC was a failure because he had no cavalry to combat the English horsemen. However, he

Below: This model of a horse-drawn chariot dates to 700BC which was at the height of the era of the chariot. Note how small the horses were. (*Ronald Sheridan*)

returned the following year with a cavalry of 2000 and was decisive in his conquest of Britain.

In the fifth century AD the major threat to the security of the Byzantine Empire (the Eastern part of the Roman Empire) emerged in the form of the cavalry forces of the Huns. Under the infamous Attila, the Huns galloped out of the bleakness of Mongolia, wreaking havoc as far as Italy and Gaul, and Attila became known as 'the scourge of God' because of the devastation his armies caused in the Roman Empire. The Hun's horsemanship was aided by a simple invention – the stirrup. The stirrup enabled them to ride faster and for a longer time, to be able to shoot their arrows more effectively and, for the cavalries which quickly copied this idea, to carry more arms and armour.

In the seventh century another threat to the Empire emerged. This was the Arabs, whose great leader was the Prophet Mohammed. He made the horse a pillar of his campaign to spread the Islamic faith and expand the Moslem Empire. The horse used, however, was not the stocky Mongolian pony of the Huns, but the fast, elegant Arab. The

Below: Alexander the Great depicted in a floor mosaic at the battle of Issus where he defeated Darius. Alexander was one of the world's most famous horsemen and he relied heavily on his cavalry for his numerous conquests. (*Peter Newark's Historical Pictures*)

71

Right: As horses were bred larger and stronger, so could they carry more armour to protect them and their riders. (*British Library*)

Right: As horses were bred larger and stronger, so could they carry more armour to protect them and their riders. (*British Library*)

Arab was given a place of honour in Islam, and its qualities helped Mohammed to develop the brilliant light cavalry that burst out of Arabia to conquer Egypt, North Africa, Spain and as far as the Loire Valley in France. It finally took a wall of infantrymen clad in chain mail to stop his forces at the Battle of Tours near Poitiers in AD732.

The light mobile cavalry used by the Huns, Arabs and their imitators was superseded in the Middle Ages by increasingly heavily armoured knights mounted on larger and larger horses, capable of standing up to any wall of infantrymen. The first time such a force made an impact in Britain was in 1066 when William the Conqueror landed with a 1000-strong heavy cavalry. The Saxons, who still used their horses for hunting rather than war, were unable to withstand such a force; they had to yield to the 'great horses' (also known as *destrier*) and their heavily armoured knights. It was the start of a new era in warfare. The armour worn by the knights became heavier and heavier and the horses were bred for size and strength. The knight and his horse became the supreme fighting machine.

It should be noted that one light mobile cavalry was still successful in the thirteenth century, for that great, but cruel, cavalry general Genghis Khan led enormous forces of Mongolians on shaggy dun ponies out of his country and conquered territory as far west as the Caspian Sea.

Knights in armour were not very manoeuvrable and ran into problems. At the battle of Crécy in 1346 the English archers, armed with a devastating new weapon, the longbow, which could shoot half a dozen arrows to the crossbow's one, destroyed the Frankish knights. The answer to the long bow was heavier armour, so during the fourteenth and fifteenth centuries plate armour which could deflect arrows replaced mail. Eventually even the horses were armoured so that a knight's charger might have to carry a ten-stone (63kg) man, eight stone (51kg) of arms and armour, a heavy saddle, and the horse's own armour, which amounted in all to about thirty stone (191kg).

For a while this sort of heavy immobile fighting force was fashionable, but problems arose with the invention of gunpowder. The first cannon was used in the fourteenth century and a hand gun called an *arquebut* in the fifteenth century. Both weapons were originally very crude and as much of a danger to the user as to the enemy. It was not really until the invention of the flint-lock musket that the firearm became manageable as a weapon. However, the musket's range was short: just enough to prevent a swordsman or lancer from charging too close, and this was sufficient to persuade the cavalry to adopt firearms. Their limitations meant that they had to be used in a way that suited the heavy horses – the cavalry trotted forward, fired, then wheeled around and retreated a little to reload.

This was a common style of warfare until well into the seventeenth century, but there were indications that better use might be made of one of the horse's major attributes – its mobility. In eastern Europe the Magyars had been successful with lightning attacks and Prince Rupert at the Battle of Edgehill used his cavalry to charge without pistols. Marlborough gave swords rather than pistols to his 20 000-strong cavalry that helped win the Battle of Blenheim. Then a maestro emerged to take full advantage of the horse's speed and manoeuvrability: this was Frederick the Great.

Frederick the Great mounted his Prussian cavalry on light, agile horses, developing the Trakehner breed for this purpose. He imposed great discipline on his soldiers, teaching them to charge sword in hand, and the result was an extremely effective striking force that won him most of his battles. Others followed his example, so that the eighteenth century saw the discarding of pistols and the rise of light, mobile cavalries. Frederick the Great's ingenuity with horses did not end there for he also developed the first really manoeuvrable horse artillery: mobile cannons drawn by six horses to provide support for his cavalry.

These were the tactics used in the Napoleonic Wars, when sadly many horses were killed. Two horses, however, emerged as great heroes. One was Marengo, an Arab stallion acquired in the Egyptian and Syrian campaigns, who allegedly carried Napoleon in all his battles from 1800 to 1815 and, after capture at Waterloo, ended his days in England. The other was Copenhagen, a 15.1hh chestnut Thoroughbred whose grandsire was the unbeaten racehorse Eclipse, and who carried Wellington at Waterloo.

The cavalry charge was taken to its saddest extreme in the Charge of the Light Brigade at Balaclava in October 1854. 670 men charged down a narrow two-mile valley to break the Russian guns. This they achieved in just twenty minutes of highly disciplined action, but the cost was 113 killed and 134 wounded men, and 470 killed and 42 wounded horses.

The cavalry was an important force in the USA, especially as a means of fighting the Indians. General Custer's stand on the Little Bighorn river in Southern Montana in June 1876 rivals the Charge of the Light Brigade for futility. Then Custer's unsupported Seventh regiment

Left: Sgt Ewart of the Scots Greys captures the Imperial Eagle standard of the 45th Regiment at Waterloo, where the cavalry played a major part. (*Peter Newark's Historical Pictures*)

Above: Napoleon riding the Arab stallion Marengo at Wagram. Allegedly this famous horse was his charger from 1800–1815. (*Peter Newark's Historical Pictures*)

Above: The Indian cavalry developed into one of the best. This is the 3rd Madras Light Cavalry of the 1880s in an impressive Review Order. (*Peter Newark's Historical Pictures*)

attacked some 3000 Sioux and Cheyenne warriors. Every man was slaughtered and only one horse, Comanche, survived. For years after Comanche appeared saddled but riderless at Seventh Cavalry Parades.

The horse probably made its greatest impact in America when the continent was first discovered by Europeans. Christopher Columbus carried horses on his second voyage in 1492 and Cortes landed in Mexico with sixteen horses. Both found them invaluable as weapons of war, for the natives were petrified and fled at the sight of these strange creatures. The invaders did not profit from this fear for long, for when the Indians acquired their own horses they turned out to be great mounted warriors and were able to slow down the advance of the Europeans.

The horse was still playing a valuable part in warfare up to and

Pages 74/75, below centre: The Indian relied largely on capturing wild horses for their mounts. This Comanche Indian is the subject of a painting by George Catlin. (*Peter Newark's Western Americana*)

Page 75, centre: A scene from the Bayeux tapestry showing the Norman cavalry leaving Hastings to go north and fight Harold. (*Ronald Sheridan*)

including World War I. Draught horses were used for moving guns and there were more than a million cavalry horses poised for action in case of a break through in the trench warfare. The first appearance of the tank heralded the end of the horse's usefulness in war. The swansong of the British cavalry was the 1917–18 Palestinian Campaign. Horses played a vital part in Allenby's victory over the Turkish Army and were involved in several brave and successful charges.

Most of the cavalries in the world ran down their horsepower after World War I – except Poland who by 1939 had mechanized only three of her forty-one cavalry regiments. When the country was invaded, the gallant soldiers charged to total disaster. For example, the Pomeranian Cavalry Brigade lost nearly 2000 of its 3000 horses in thirty minutes.

The Russians too, maintained some mounted cavalry divisions. They played a useful part in worrying the Germans in their advance towards Moscow, but what is believed to be the last full-scale cavalry charge was another disaster. In 1941 at the village of Musino 2000 members of the 44th Mongolian Cavalry Division charged the Germans. They were mown down in just ten minutes and not a single German died.

The horse's role as an instrument of war is over. His contribution is now largely confined to giving man pleasure; and the challenge of controlling this extraordinary creature and working in harmony with it remains undiminished.

For centuries man has been devising better ways of making best use of the horse, and the history of the development of equitation is as fascinating as the horse's role in war.

The development of horsemanship

Man was quick to see the possibilities of using the horse for sport and by 676BC it had its first competition at the Olympic Games. It was a chariot race, but ridden activities were introduced later. It is questionable how much training would help in the rough, exciting sport of chariot racing but attempts were made, for in the Kikkuli Text, dated about 1360BC, detailed instruction on the driving of chariots is given.

The ancient Greeks were probably the first to practise the more sophisticated form of riding – High School – for on the Parthenon Frieze there are horses in advanced movements – the *levade* and *piaffe*. They produced, too, one of the greatest equestrian writers of all time: Xenophon, whose essays on horsemanship, *Hippike*, translated and collected by Professor Morris-Morgan in *The Art of Horsemanship by Xenophon*, is one of the most often quoted equestrian books in the world. It is so full of common sense and the arguments are so logically produced, that much of the contents remain valid today.

The Greeks produced some excellent art and literature on the horse, but the most important invention of the era is attributed to the Celts, who in the third century BC started using a bit which looked very similar to today's snaffle, and even more important, the curb. The curb bit which brought pressure to bear on the chin groove meant that some of the horrific contraptions (spiked mouthpieces, etc.) could be discarded, but not everyone did so.

The Romans were practical horsemen. There is no evidence of them practising the sophisticated High School riding of the Greek era. There is no literature about how to ride in a classical style, only on the more

Left: A warrior of the Nez
Percé tribe. This tribe was
famed for its horsemanship
and was responsible for
developing the Appaloosa
breed. (*Peter Newark's
Western Americana*)

mundane subject of stable management. It was in Roman times, however, that three important innovations were made. The first was the
horseshoe, which was invented about AD100 and enabled horses to be
worked all year round and on rough surfaces. The second was the
saddle tree, which made riding more comfortable and secure than
riding bareback or on saddlecloths. It also provided the support needed
for the most important but simple invention – the stirrup. It was in the
fifth century that the Huns were first seen using this great aid to riding.

The invention of the stirrup heralded the next era in horsemanship –
that of the knights who were so heavily protected and immobile that
they would have toppled off without the stirrup. The horses became
heavier and larger to transport this weight, and skills of horsemanship
seemed to have been confined to strength and steering a straight line.

These skills were tested to the full in the tournaments when combats

Above: These heavily armoured and decoratively clad jousting knights are depicted in the Military Roll of Arms. (*Ronald Sheridan*)

were staged between teams at first (a *mêlée*), then just two individuals (a *joust*). The tournaments embodied all the glories and dangers of war without some of the discomforts like dirt, disease or flies. The custom was for the knight to fight in honour of a selected lady, and, if he won, her favours were his, regardless of whether she was married. To win he would have to survive the terrific shock of meeting an opponent's lance point when both horses were at full gallop and he had to keep his horse running straight so that he could aim effectively with his own lance.

It was rather pedantic horsemanship, but the great change came with the Renaissance. In the spirit of the time rational thought could be said to have been applied to equestrianism as well as to art and literature. The first great master of such an approach was the Neapolitan nobleman, Federico Grisone, who in 1532 founded a riding academy in Naples. There he taught young noblemen horsemanship, but by revolutionary methods using reason and logic to teach the horse to carry out complicated movements at slow, dramatic paces – this was the start of scholastic riding.

In 1550 Grisone wrote a book in which he explained his ideas. It was a huge success. Young aristocrats flocked to his school, other instructors followed his methods to start their own academies, and this led to the development of what became known as the Neapolitan School. Foreigners started to attend and the fashion for this exotic and intellectual form of riding spread quickly across Europe. High School became an essential part of any ambitious young man's education and the courts of the civilized world built *manèges* to ride in, and to stage regular equestrian displays.

Grisone showed that an intelligent approach to riding was successful, but force still played an essential part in the horse's education. If a

horse did not obey it was assumed that this was due to stubbornness rather than to lack of ability or understanding, so punishment was the answer. From the time of Grisone to the present day, however, a series of great riding masters gradually proved the falsity of this basic concept. They devised methods to improve the horse's ability and his understanding so that he could learn progressively how to do difficult movements without force being applied, except for reprimands when he was mischievous.

Evolution was gradual. Many of the Italian instructors went abroad and taught others who then improved on the methods. One named Chevalier Saint Antoine came to England and aroused an interest in the art, which was furthered by Britain's one and only great master of High School, William Cavendish, Duke of Newcastle.

The Duke, born in 1592, was a man of many talents other than riding. He was an important person in Charles I's court and was tutor to the Prince of Wales until the Civil War forced him to flee. He settled in Antwerp where he set up a riding academy which rapidly became famous. On one occasion he was said to have demonstrated to some Spanish visitors who 'crossed themselves' and cried 'Miracule!'.

With the Restoration, Newcastle returned to England to lead the only important period of High School in a country dominated by sporting rather than academic riders. His two most important contributions to riding were the invention of the draw rein – an additional rein running from the girth through the bit to the hand, which is used by many show jumpers today; he also reduced the amount of force needed in training, saying in one of his books, 'A boy is a long time before he knows his alphabet, longer before he has learn'd to spell, and several years before he can read distinctly; and yet there are some people who, as soon as they have got upon a young horse, entirely undressed or untaught, fancy that by beating and spurring they will make him a dress'd horse in one morning only.'

Newcastle was Britain's lone champion of High School. English court

Above: Fighting in the Middle Ages was not solely for the purposes of entertainment. Here, Bruce kills Sir Henry Bohun, as depicted in the 14th century 'Chronicle of England'. (*Mary Evans Picture Library*)

life was not as exotic as on the Continent and the *carrousels* and parades were never as popular as hunting. The closest the British came to High School riding after Newcastle was in the circus. The greatest of the eighteenth century British riders – Philip Astley – produced a book describing his methods, but he gained few converts because the British were mad about racing and hunting. The French nineteenth-century writer Picard's description of the British is apt: 'The horsemen have an incontestable boldness but no method.'

High School, however, had plenty of devotees, especially the French who were the leaders in equitation from the seventeenth to the nineteenth centuries. They also developed the principles of equitation which we use today. It started when two Frenchmen – Solomon de La Broue and Antoine de Pluvinel de Baume – went to Italy at the height of the Neapolitan High School fever. They returned, La Broue to write the first French book on equitation and Pluvinel to open an academy in Paris where the noblest in the land came to learn, amongst them the future king, Louis XIII. Pluvinel's famous book *La Manège Royale* (1623) is a dialogue between the two.

The French kings took to equitation and Louis XIV made his magnificent Versailles court the centre for this sport. The most famous equestrian master of all time, François Robichon, Sieur de la Guérinière, taught during his reign. The principles he established are those we use today and he paved the way for more artistic freedom of action. His aim for 'this noble and useful art . . . is solely to make horses

Opposite: A horse in *piaffe* (trotting on the spot) between pillars at the Spanish Riding School. Without the weight of the rider it is easier for the horse to remain active and yet not move forward. (*Robert Harding Associates*)

Below: A Berber horseman shows off his agility on horseback in an illustration from a seventeenth century book on equitation by Antonio d'Andrade. (*British Library*)

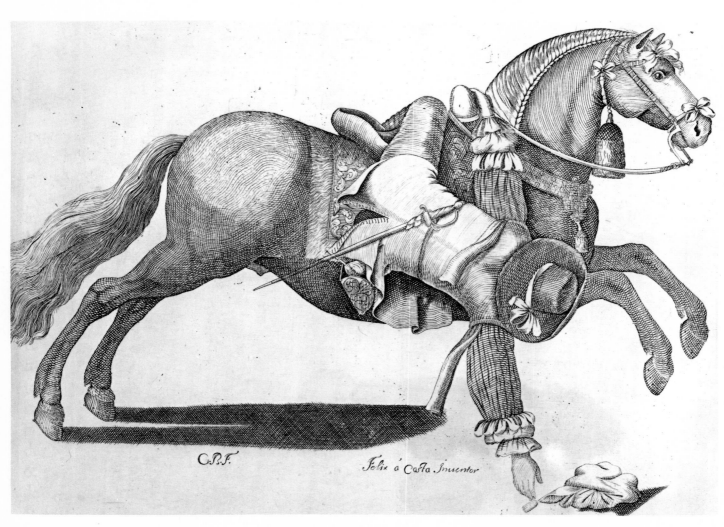

supple, loose, flexible, compliant and obedient and to lower the quarters, without all of which a horse – he may be meant for military service, hunting or dressage – will be neither comfortable in his movements, nor pleasurable to ride.'

Guérinière introduced some important movements – *the shoulder-in*, the *counter-canter*, and the *flying change*. All of these were contained in his book *Ecole de Cavalrie* (1733), and its contents are the basis for the

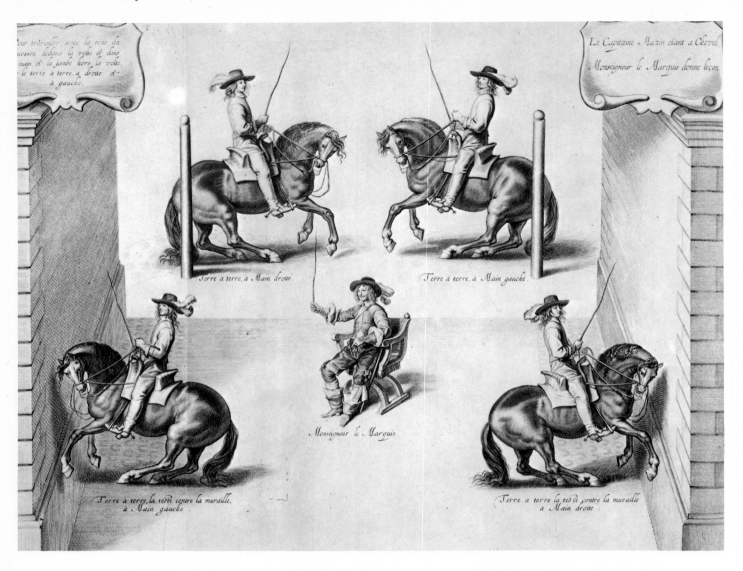

Eur tethraulet avec la reine du nesson dedans la volte et dans main, et la jambe hors la volte, le terre a terre, a droite et a gauche.

Le Capitaine Mazin étant a Cheval. Monseigneur le Marquis donne leçon.

Terre à terre, à Main droite.

Terre à terre, à Main gauche.

Monseigneur le Marquis.

Terre à terre, la teste contre la muraille, à Main gauche.

Terre à terre la teste contre la muraille à Main droite.

Above: High School riding became a fashionable activity amongst the European nobility. Britain's only great champion of this form of riding was the Duke of Newcastle, and this is an illustration from one of his books. (*Robert Harding Associates*)

only early school which remains in existence today – the Spanish Riding School in Vienna. This famous school started after the Hapsburgs imported some Spanish horses in 1572. They chose these horses because their intelligence and power made them especially suitable for the new craze of High School riding. The school has now functioned in Vienna for 400 years and can be considered a custodian of history and 'the' guardian of the art of classical riding.

The work of two further French masters in the nineteenth century made little impact on the methods of the Spanish Riding School, but they did on Russian, German and French methods. With the decline of the exotic court a riding master's life had changed from training noblemen to working in the circus, and in this sphere in the last century James Fillis and François Baucher excelled. Baucher was the first leading equitation master who was a commoner. He was able to train a horse very quickly, basing his methods on the principle of destroying a horse's instinct and will, so that he came to rely on the rider.

James Fillis supported the nineteenth century trend in dressage for forward movement and greater extension, and, although he was a circus performer, his influence spread through Europe through his beautifully written book – ghosted by the French premier Georges Clemençeau – *Principes de Dressage et d'Equitation* (1890); and for

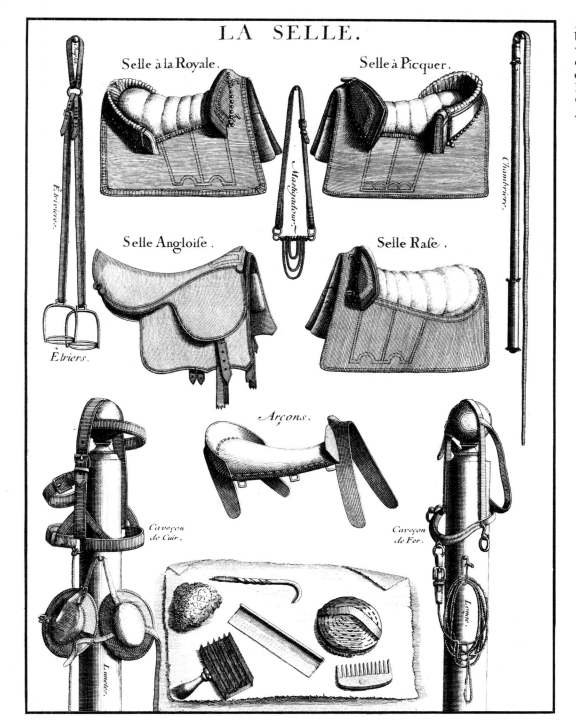

LA SELLE.

Selle à la Royale.

Selle à Picquer.

Selle Angloife.

Selle Rafe.

Étrivières.

Martingadour.

Chambriere.

Étriers.

Arçons.

Caveçon de Cuir.

Caveçon de Fer.

Longe.

Lunettes.

Left: Illustrations from the book *Ecole de Cavalrie* which was written in the eighteenth century by one of the greatest masters of High School – Sieur de la Guérinière. (*British Library*)

twelve years he was instructor to the Russian cavalry in St Petersburg.

While the Europeans were improving the art of High School in enclosed spaces, the British were galloping in races or across country after hounds. At first there were no jumps when hunting, but the Enclosure Acts changed this, and during the seventeenth century the sport of foxhunting and with it the jumping of hedges, developed.

Competitive jumping was first recorded in 1752 when two Irish gentlemen challenged each other to race to a specified point. Others thought the concept was fun, steeplechasing quickly developed, spreading to England where in 1839 the first Grand National was staged.

Jumping over fences that could be knocked down inside arenas was a later innovation, and again started in Ireland in the courtyard of the Royal Dublin Society's premises in 1864. Then they were known as

Right: After the downfall of the French court, the cavalry of the black-coated Cadre Noir took over as leaders of horsemanship. This is their spectacular *reprise des sauteurs.* (*J. Decker*)

leaping contests, the French copied the idea in 1866 and they were introduced to the Olympic Games in 1900.

The contestants in these leaping and steeplechasing events used basically the same position as in High School riding, adopting long stirrups and leaning back over the fence, which supposedly lightened the horse's forehand enabling it to leave the ground. This concept was changed by the Italian officer, Federico Caprilli (1867–1907), who claimed that this style interfered with the horse's movement. He claimed the rider should follow the horse's motion and not the rider's instinctive adjustments to gravity. To achieve this the rider should sit forward over the fence, and this becomes easier if the stirrups are shortened so that the angles of the waist, knee and ankle are reduced.

This was not as much of a revolution as is sometimes suggested, for the great American jockey, Tod Sloan, had already started racing with short stirrups and a forward seat. It was enough of an innovation, however, for many interested equestrians to flock to Italy to learn how to jump, just as they had three centuries before to learn about a scholastic approach to riding.

Caprilli's methods are less relevant today, for not only did he advocate a forward seat, but also natural gaits with little contact on the reins and no collection. Today's complicated arrangements of fences force most riders to intervene during the approach and collection is needed to jump the huge obstacles clear.

The Americans use their horses not only to jump and perform High School, but also to round up cattle and travel great distances. The Western Seat was evolved for these purposes and was introduced to the USA after the conquest of Mexico by Cortes. It is based on traditional Spanish techniques which they in turn had learnt from the Moors and the Moors from the Saracens. It is a style which has allegedly been practised for as long as classical riding. It is a practical style, for with

Left: The life of a cavalry trooper and his mount could be bleak; here one is on guard in a Montana blizzard. (*Peter Newark's Western Americana*)

Below, left: The Indians were more famed for courageous than skilful riding, as in this example where they are using their horses as shields. (*Peter Newark's Western Americana*)

the loose reins held in one hand the rider can perform other duties (lassoing, shooting, etc.), and the large saddle with a high pommel cantel gives the rider great security and comfort for long rides.

Today the various styles of riding which have evolved over the centuries are rarely used for utilitarian purposes: simply to give riders satisfaction and fun in general riding and to provide the great challenge of mastering them to the best possible degree. The test of their mastery over the horse is no longer the battlefield but the competition. Competitions have become the central feature of riding in the twentieth century and the discoveries and ideas of the masters of equitation over the ages still provide the concepts which riders must master to achieve a high standard of performance. The great master Guérinière summed it up when he said 'Without theory all practice is aimless'.

The Horse in Literature and Art

The horse in literature

The horse has been a source of inspiration to artists and writers since time immemorial. Rudyard Kipling is near to the heart of the matter when, in *The Ballad of the King's Jest*, he said:

Four things are greater than all things,
Women and Horses and Power and War.

The greatest writer of them all, William Shakespeare, however, comes closest to capturing a little of the horse's magic with this piece from *Henry V:*

When I bestride him I soar, I am a hawk he
trots the air, the earth sings when he touches it.

Equestrian literature has been found from early periods, but the first great masterpiece is that of Xenophon. He was a cavalry commander who lived in Athens 2300 years ago. Although his most remarkable work is *Anabasis*, the story of 10 000 Greek mercenaries who were defeated in the Persian Rebellion of 401BC, his most famous work in the equestrian world is his manual of horsemanship. Called *Peri Hippikes* (On the Art of Horsemanship), it contains such wonderful pieces of advice as:

The gods have given the power of instructing each other in their duties by word of mouth which is denied to a horse . . . But if you can reward him when he obeys as you wish end punish him when he is disobedient he will thus learn to know his duty. This rule can be said to apply to the whole art of horsemanship.

And:

First, then, it must be realised that spirit in a horse is precisely what anger is in a man. Therefore, just as you are least likely to make a man angry if you neither say nor do anything disagreeable to him, so he who abstains from annoying a spirited horse is least likely to rouse his anger.

With the fall of the Greek Empire the horse became a more utilitarian creature, the subject of practical but not romantic or great literature. Shakespeare corrected this trend in his first major work *Venus and Adonis*:

Sometimes he trots, as if he told the steps
With gentle majesty and modest pride;
Anon he rears upright, curvets and leaps
As who should say, 'Lo, thus my strength is tried . . .

Round hoof'd, short jointed, fetlocks shag and long,
Broad breast, full eye, small head and nostril wide,
High crest, short ears, straight legs and passing strong,
Thin mane, thick tail, broad buttock, tender hide . . .

A rather less romantic view of the horse was taken by foxhunting's most famous author, Robert Surtees (1803–1864), who is, at times, rather rude about the beast who carried his colourful cockney heroes cross country. In *Handley Cross* we get such references as 'Come Hup! I say, you hugly beast!' – and 'Con-found all presents wot eat!' But he did understand the relationship between horse and man for he also says in *Mr Sponge's Sporting Tour*: 'There is no secret so close as that between a rider and his horse.' And he really did understand the emotions associated with hunting, as is shown in the often quoted piece from *Handley Cross:*

Unting is all that's worth living for – all time is lost wot is not spent in hunting – it is like the hair we breathe – if we have it not we die – its the sport of kings, the image of war without its guilt, and only five-and-twenty per cent of its danger.

Then in *Mr Sponge's Sporting Tour* we get this vivid description of when the hounds find the fox:

There was such an outburst of melody, and such a shaking of the gorse bushes as plainly showed there was no safety for Reynard in cover; and

87

great was the bustle and commotion among the horsemen. Mr Fossick lowered his hat-string and ran the fox's tooth through the button hole; Fyle drew his girths; Washball took a long swig at his hunting horn-shaped monkey; Major Mark and Mr Archer threw away their cigar ends; Mr Bliss drew his dogskin gloves; Mr Wake rolled the thong of his whip round the stick, to be better able to encounter his puller; Mr Sparke got a yokel to take up a link of his curb; George Smith and Joe Smith looked at their watches; Sandy McGregor, the factor, filled his great Scots nose with Irish snuff, exclaiming, as he dismissed the balance from his fingers by a knock against his thigh, 'Oh, my mon, aw think this tod will gie us a run!', while Blossomnose might be seen stealing gently forward, on the far side of a thick fence, for the double purpose of shirking Jawleyford, and getting a good start.

In the midst of these and similar preparations for the fray, up went a whip's cap at the low end of the cover; and a volley of 'Tally-hos' burst from our friends, as for the fox, whisking his white-tipped brush in the air, was seen stealing away over the grassy hill beyond. What a commotion was there! How pale some looked. How happy others!

Surtees' humorous books were such a success in the 1830s that another publisher commissioned a young writer called Dickens to write a similar sort of work. The result was *Pickwick Papers* in which we get some even more colourful characters (although at the time supporters were pretty equally divided between Pickwick and Jorrocks). The horse does not play such an important role in Dickens' work, but they are the central figures in one very funny chapter when Mr Pickwick undertook to drive and Mr Winkle to ride:

Mr Winkle pulled at the bridle of the tall horse till he was black in the face; and having at length succeeded in stopping him, dismounted, handed the whip to Mr Pickwick, and grasping the reins, prepared to remount.

Now whether the tall horse, in the natural playfulness of his disposition, was desirous of having a little innocent recreation with Mr Winkle, or whether it occurred to him that he could perform the journey as much to his own satisfaction without a rider as with one, are points upon which, of course, we can arrive at no definite and distinct conclusion. By whatever motives the animal was actuated certain it is that Mr Winkle had no sooner touched the reins than he slipped them over his head, and darted backwards to their full length.

'Poor fellow', said Mr Winkle, soothingly – 'Poor fellow – good old horse.'
The 'poor fellow' was proof against flattery; the more Mr Winkle tried to get
nearer him, the more he sidled away: and notwithstanding all kinds of
coaxing and wheedling, there was Mr Winkle and the horse going round and
round each other for ten minutes, at the end of which time each was at
precisely the same distance from the other as when they first commenced –
an unsatisfactory sort of thing under any circumstances, and particularly so
in a lonely road, where no assistance can be procured.

Tolstoy, one of the world's greatest masters of descriptive prose, was
a rider and the horse often plays a part in his works, but it is his
description in *Anna Karenina* of Count Vronsky's ride on Frou-Frou in
a steeplechase that is probably most memorable:

Vronsky could hear Gladiator's gallop and puffing coming nearer. He
spurred his horse and could feel with joy how she quickened her speed, and
the distance between her and Gladiator was again increased.

He now had the lead as he had desired and as Cord had recommended and
felt certain of success. His excitement, his joy and tenderness for Frou-Frou
increased. He wanted to look back, but dared not, and tried to calm himself
and not to spur his horse too much, so as to reserve her energy. The most
difficult jump was still before him; if he could clear that first he was sure to
win the race. They drew near to the Irish bank. Both he and Frou-Frou could
see it from a distance, and each felt a moment of hesitation. Vronsky noticed
the hesitation in his horse's ears, but instantly felt that she regained her
confidence and knew exactly what to do. She made a tremendous effort, rose
in the air, and with one bound cleared the bank and the ditch together and
went on without changing the measure of her pace.

The most famous book on a horse is, unlike *Anna Karenina*, not a great
book. It is, however, an entrancing, touchingly simple work which has
enraptured millions of readers and helped in the last century to draw
attention to, and get something done about, the ill-treatment to horses.
The writer was an invalid – Anna Sewell. She had the work published
just over a hundred years ago (1877) and the book was *Black Beauty*. It
is written in the first person with Black Beauty recounting a long series
of adventures under different owners. This is a description of the first
home to cause him some discomfort:

Hitherto I had always been driven by people who at least knew how to drive;
but in this place I was to get my experience of all the different kinds of bad
and ignorant driving to which we horses are subjected; for I was a 'job-
horse', and was let out to all sorts of people who wished to hire me; and as I
was good-tempered and gentle, I think I was more often let out to the
ignorant drivers than some of the other horses, because I could be depended
upon. It would take a long time to tell of all the different styles in which I
was driven, but I will mention a few of them.

First, there were the tight-rein drivers – men who seemed to think that all
depended on holding the reins as hard as they could, never relaxing the pull
on the horse's mouth or giving him the least liberty of movement. These are
always talking about 'keeping the horse well in hand', and 'holding a horse
up', just as if a horse was not made to hold himself up. Some poor broken-
down horses, whose mouths have been made hard and insensible by just such

89

drivers as these, may, perhaps, find some support in it; but for a horse who can depend upon its own legs, has a tender mouth, and is easily guided, it is not only tormenting, but stupid.

Then there are the loose-rein drivers . . .

This century there have been some distinguished poets who have concentrated on equestrian subjects. John Masefield was a Poet Laureate and his book *Right Royal*, in which he describes a victory in a steeplechase, is valued by all who enjoy racing:

And smiting the turf to clods that scattered
Was the rush of the race, the thing that mattered,
A tide of horses in fury flowing,

Beauty of speed in glory going,
Kubbadar pulling, romping first,
Like a big black fox that had made his burst.

And away and away and away they went,
A visible song of what life meant.
Living in houses, sleeping in bed,
Going to business, all seemed dead,
Dead as death to that rush in strife,
Pulse for pulse with the heart of life.

'For to all', Charles thought, 'when the blood beats high
Comes the glimpse of that which may not die;
When the world is stilled, when the wanting dwindles,
When the mind takes light and the spirit kindles,
One stands on a peak of this old earth'.

Below: The massiveness of the fences which Right Royal had to jump in John Masefield's moving work is well illustrated by Cecil Alden. (*Heinemann, 1922*)

Left: Fire terrifies horses and Alice B. Woodward has captured Black Beauty's fear in this illustration for Anna Sewell's book. (*G Bell & Sons, 1931*)

Below, left: An illustration from John Masefield's *Right Royal* by Cecil Alden. (*Heinemann, 1922*)

Below: A sketch by Alice B. Woodward from Anna Sewell's *Black Beauty* which captures some of the simplicity and charm of this famous book. (*G Bell & Sons, 1931*)

Then there was the New Zealander, Will H. Ogilvie, who wrote some stirring poems mainly about hunting and racing:

Who dreams to go god-like must gallop perforce,
So buckle my spur, put the gear on my horse,
Give me grass for his hoofs and the wind in his mane,
A call to the skyline and homeward again.

Of the books this century, although I have spent many happy hours with Donn Byrn's *Destiny Bay*, the pride of place must go to Siegfried Sassoon's *Memoirs of a Fox-Hunting Man*. Sassoon was also a poet and he wrote some refreshing descriptions of his youth when so much of his time was devoted to racing and hunting horses. This is a vivid description of early mornings cubhunting:

The mornings I remember most zestfully were those which took us up on to the chalk downs. To watch the day breaking from purple to dazzling gold while we trotted up a deep-rutted lane; to inhale the early freshness when we were on the sheep-cropped uplands; to stare back at the low country with its cock-crowing farms and mist-cooled waterways; thus to be riding out with a sense of spacious discovery – was it not something stolen from the lie-a-bed world and the luckless city worker – even though it ended in nothing more than the killing of a leash of fox-cubs.

That was a wonderful appreciation of the country and the riding, but it is an American writer, Mason Houghland, who in *Gone Away* produced one of the most creditable explanations of the lure of foxhunting:

Foxhunting is not merely a sport – and it is more nearly a passion than a game. It is a religion, a racial faith. In it are the elements that form the framework upon which beliefs are built; the attempt to escape from life as it is to a life as we would have it; an abiding love of beauty; and an unconscious search for the eternal verities of fair play, loyalty and sympathetic accord, which are so clouded in our mundane existence.

It is a primitive faith, a 'survival' the sociologist would term it, and harks back to the clear and simple outlook of our tribal gods. Through the years it goes on because, after the flush of many dawns, the thrill of never-ending pursuit, the sweet spice of danger, the simple tragedies of the field, and the weary darkness of long roads home, a few always become attuned to Nature's wondrous harmony of which they themselves are a part.

No great books have been written on the horses that are so popular in these post-war years – the show jumpers and competition horses – although both Lucinda Prior-Palmer in *Up, Up and Away* and Pat Smythe in *Jump for Joy* did capture a little of the emotion and excitement of their sport. I think the most important piece of recent years is that of the poet and prose writer, Ronald Duncan. It is also as a tribute to the horse and an appropriate piece on which to end the discussion on literature and pass on to art:

Where in this wide world can man find nobility without pride,
Friendship without envy,
Or beauty without vanity?

Here, where grace is laced with muscle,
And strength by gentleness confined.
He serves without servility;
He has fought without emnity.
There is nothing so powerful,
Nothing less violent,
There is nothing so quick,
Nothing more patient,
England's past has been borne on his back.
All our history is his industry.
We are his heirs, he is our inheritance,
The Horse.

Above, left: A striking
illustration of the huntsman
and his hounds which was
the work of William
Nicholson and appeared in
Siegfried Sassoon's *Memoirs
of a Fox-Hunting Man.*
(Faber & Faber Ltd, 1929)

Above, right: Another of
William Nicholson's
illustrations from *Memoirs
of a Fox-Hunting Man*
which conveys a little of the
thrill of jumping natural
fences. *(Faber & Faber Ltd,
1929)*

The horse in art

The oldest efforts by man to depict the horse are the rock drawings and
engravings of the prehistoric horse, which date from approximately
30 000 to 10 000BC. There are over seventy grottos with such paintings
and engravings in France, and thirty-three in Spain, but probably the
most exciting of these are the painted pictures of Lascaux in the Dor-
dogne. The caves having been hermetically sealed by nature meant the
paint had retained its original brilliance.

The Greeks have given us some of the earliest equestrian master-
pieces. In the world of sculpture the most famous is the Parthenon
Frieze of the Acropolis, built between 447 and 406BC, when Xenophon

119   120   121   122

Left, above: The earliest paintings of horses were those found on cave walls like these from Altimira in Spain. (*Michael Holford*)

Left, below: These magnificent horses performing High School movements are part of Athens' Parthenon frieze. (*Michael Holford*)

Below: The horses of San Marco, Venice have travelled the world, originally as the spoils of war, and now to be exhibited in major cities. (*Ronald Sheridan*)

was writing his books. It is a magnificent relief depicting a procession of Athenians, both mounted and in chariots, and it can be seen today in the British Museum.

Another civilization to produce great works on the horse was the Eastern Han Dynasty (AD25–220). There is a magnificent jade carving of a horse's head in the Victoria and Albert Museum from this period, but some of the most exciting finds were only made in 1969 when the tomb of a high official was unearthed. In it were 230 artefacts, mainly horses, which are now on display in the Exhibition of Cultural Relics in Peking.

Probably the most famous horse sculptures are the four horses of St Mark's in Venice. Cast in an amalgam of copper, silver and gold, they are magnificent, elegant works. Despite weighing 1700 lbs (772kg) they have been stolen or taken as the 'spoils of victory' to be displayed all over Europe. Their temporary homes have included Trojan's Arch in Rome, Constantinople and Paris to which they were taken by Napoleon. Their origin is not certain, but it is believed that they were a Roman copy of a Greek sculpture and are thought to have been brought from Chios to Constantinople in the fifth century AD.

The horse has always been a symbol of superiority and power, and great generals and kings frequently chose to be painted or sculpted when riding. The first great statue of a horse and rider is that of Marcus Aurelius, which stands in the Piazza del Campidoglio in Rome, and was

Above: Donatello's magnificent equestrian statue of Gattamelata which stands in the Piazza del Santo in Padua. (*Alinari*)

Above, right: St George was a popular subject in the late Middle Ages and this outstanding version was created by Dürer. (*British Library*)

finished in AD173. It is huge, standing seventeen feet (5 metres) high and has provided inspiration to the sculptors of later years.

After this magnificent effort, the horse suffered a lean period as an artistic subject and it was not until the fifteenth century that it was treated seriously again. One particularly noble statue stands in Padua. It is the work of Donatello, the Tuscan sculptor who was commissioned in 1443 to produce this monument to General Gattemalata. He was a Venetian general, as was Colleoni, whose more dynamic monument on his horse was sculpted a few years later by Verrocchio and stands in Venice.

The most impressive, however, are works by Giovanni Lorenzo Bernini (1598–1680). His two superb equestrian statues were completed towards the end of his life and the subjects were Constantine, the first Christian Emperor, and the French King, Louis XIV. The statue of Constantine stands in the Vatican in Rome and portrays in dramatic fashion the moment of his conversion in AD211 when he saw the Cross in the sky. His horse is rearing and his hands are outstretched and few people can look at it without emotion. The statue of Louis XIV, is more conventional and has less impact, but is nevertheless one of the great equestrian statues.

In London one of the most pleasing equestrian statues is Matthew Cotes Wyatt's bronze of George III on his favourite charger, Adonis. It stands near to Trafalgar Square.

Of the modern sculptors, John Skeaping stands out: of special interest are his life-size works of the great sire, Hyperion, which is at Newmarket and that of the impressive Derby winner, Mill Reef.

Painters have, since prehistoric times, chosen the horse as a subject, but it became especially popular in the Renaissance. Along with the revival of arts and letters began a vogue for High School riding – a

revival and development of the classical ways of riding used by the Greeks. The horse became a status symbol, a source of prestige and splendour and the subject of many great paintings. Raphael, one of the three great creators of Renaissance art, painted a magnificent cream-coloured charger in his depiction of St George and the Dragon, which now stands in the Louvre.

The painters of this time used the horse to magnify the power and stature of kings and leaders. Titian (1487–1576) did just this for Emperor Charles V mounted on his charger at the Battle of Mühlberg. Van Dyck painted Charles I on an elegant, grand horse which tends to heighten rather than take away from the majesty of the king. This great picture hangs in the National Gallery.

Velázquez (1599–1660), a Spaniard, was even able to give stature to a child on a horse, for in his pictures of the Infante Don Balthasar Carlos in the Riding School (one of which is in the Wallace Collection, London) the young infant already looks an accomplished horseman, relaxed and dignified, with his pony in a half-rear. Velázquez also completed an even more regal portrait of Philip IV on horseback, which hangs in the Prado, Madrid.

The horse continued to be used as a means of magnifying the importance of the human subject, but a new development in equestrian art occurred in the eighteenth century, with the British School of sporting art, when the horse became the equal of, or even more important than his rider. Although this school had Continental origins, for it was the Flemish and Dutch painters who came to Britain at the end of the seventeenth century who sowed the seeds, it was essentially a British art form. Between 1725 and 1860 British artists produced a long series of paintings of hunting, racing, coaching and portraits of the equine heroes of the period. The only other country to take up this School of

Above: Goya completed a series on bullfighting which now hangs in the Biblioteca Naçional, Madrid. This is the third composition, 'The Death of Pepe Lillo'. (*Biblioteca Naçional, Madrid*)

97

Several facets of the horse's role in relation to men as depicted by different artists –

Right: The American artist D M Russell's painting 'Flying Hoofs' showing wild horses keeping wolves at bay. (*Peter Newark's Western Americana*)

Opposite, above: An elegant picture of a phaeton harnessed up to a pair of cream ponies by the great eighteenth century animal painter George Stubbs. (*Cooper-Bridgeman*)

Below: Much of the atmosphere of life out West was captured by Frederic Remington's work like this one of 'The Coming and Going of the Pony Express'. (*Peter Newark's Western Americana*)

Opposite, below: The twentieth century artist John Skeaping is famous for the action depicted in his work. These racehorses are typical examples. (*Fotomas Index*)

art was America. The emigrés, Edward Troye (1808–1874) and Arthur Fitzwilliam Tait (1819–1905) introduced the concept and influenced such well-known painters of the racehorse and racing scenes as Henry Stull and Frederic Remington, although the latter extended his equine interest to cover a more American subject – the Wild West.

The greatest exponent of the British School of sporting art was George Stubbs (1724–1806). Born in Liverpool, he started as a portrait painter before becoming interested in anatomy. He spent much time dissecting carcasses before producing his brilliant book *The Anatomy of the Horse*. His understanding of anatomy enabled him to paint realistically and refreshingly, and this won him many patrons in the 1760s when racing, foxhunting and the Thoroughbred were developing so quickly. Stubbs was the painter who led the trend in painting away from the portrait, the aggrandizement of rank and power, to depictions of rural life.

His patrons commissioned him to paint portraits of horses and dogs or of hunting and racing scenes, and he also painted a beautiful series of pictures of horses and mares grazing in tranquil landscapes. But he was much more than an animal portrait painter, for he portrayed nature in a simple, accurate and exceptionally distinguished manner.

Stubbs was a genius, but he was not the founder of the British School, for Francis Barlow (1626–1702), Peter Tillemans (1684–1734) and John Wootton (1686–1765) were the fathers of the movement. Commissioned by the nobility and gentry, they portrayed sedate hunting or racing subjects, but with fussy decorations. James Seymour (1702–1752), also Stubbs' peer, took to painting after losing his money on the turf.

George Morland (1763–1804), like Stubbs, left to us accurate and beautiful representations of English country life. He was the son of the painter Henry Morland, who has two pictures in the National Gallery. His father quickly recognized the talents of his son, put him to work, and at ten he exhibited at the Royal Academy. An allegedly cruel apprenticeship of seven years under his father followed, when he was forced to work desperately hard with no reward. When released from these ties he alternated between a life of debauchery – race-riding, accumulating debts – and painting a prolific number of works which, in later years, were usually snapped up by debt collectors.

James Ward (1769–1859), who became George Morland's brother-in-law, is often considered to be the greatest painter of horses, as he not only gives an accurate representation of their physical features, but also of their character. He used these talents to portray two of the most famous in history – Napoleon's charger, Marengo, and the Duke of Wellington's Copenhagen.

There were numerous artists who contributed to this voluminous production of sporting art. Probably the best was Benjamin Marshall (1767–1835) who many rate second only to Stubbs; Henry Alken (1786–1851) who depicted the exploits of hard-riding squires and huntsmen; J. F. Herring (1795–1865), who started as a stage coachman and taught himself to paint; John Ferneley (1782–1860), a pupil of Ben Marshall, who painted from the centre of the hunting country at Melton Mowbray; and James Pollard (1792–1867) who was a prolific producer of coaching, hunting and racing scenes, many of which went into prints.

Probably the greatest painter of this period was the Frenchman, Eugène Delacroix (1789–1863) who was the major painter of the

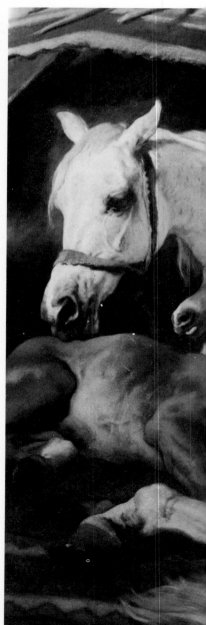

Below: A detail from Landseer's tender and decorative portrayal of an Arab mare and her foal. (*Reproduced by permission of the Trustees, the Wallace Collection, London*)

Romantic movement in France. Horses were a recurrent theme in his pictures – not in the sporting nature of the British artists, but in the heroic, majestic manner of artists of earlier eras. His horses are usually the prancing or rearing mounts of the great men he wished to portray.

Of the Impressionist painters, it was Degas who showed the greatest mastery in the depiction of the horse. He was able to catch unusual moments and convey a strong sense of movement in his horses and their jockeys.

The outstanding equestrian artist of the twentieth century was Sir Alfred Munnings, P.R.A. (1879–1959). He was a conventional artist, famous for his outspoken attacks on modern art; he even referred to Matisse and Cézanne as 'foolish daubers'. His paintings of everything from cart to race horses are simple and beautiful memorials to them and the countryside. Of the modern artists, the most famous must be John Skeaping, R.A., born 1901, who has forsaken accurate representation to convey speed, excitement and so much of the exhilaration of the sports in which the horse is the vital feature.

Below: Goya's elegant portrait of Queen Maria Luisa on horseback hangs in Madrid's Prado Museum. *(Museo del Prado, Madrid)*

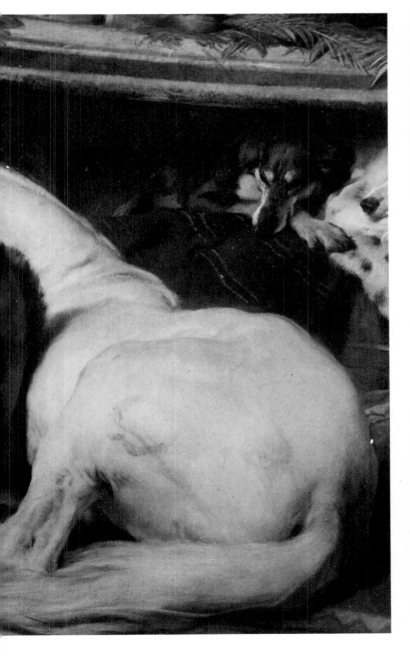

Right: Hunting started as a means for man to fill his larder and this rather than pleasure was the reason these Sioux hunted buffalo. (*Peter Newark's Western Americana*)

The Horse in Sport

Hunting

Hunting with horses started as a practical activity – a means for man to fill his larder. The exhilaration of the chase was so great, however, that royalty, emperors and aristocrats took to it as sport. Only edible animals – in particular the stag – were pursued at first, but in the eighteenth century foxhunting, which was a faster form of hunting and involved jumping fences, became more popular. In the last hundred years an artificial form of hunting – draghunting – has also become more common. In this form of hunting a man-made scent keeps the hounds running.

Staghunting is the oldest form of hunting in existence today. There is some evidence that it was practised in prehistoric times, but we know that the Anglo-Saxons and nobility of the Middle Ages were ardent participants. The heavily forested lands of France and England abounded with deer which were chased by rather heavy, slow hounds and sportsmen on equally pedantic, sturdy horses. The French speeded up the sport by breeding faster hounds, and James I introduced this more exciting form of staghunting to England. It wasn't long, however, before forests were thinned out and deer became rarer. In the eighteenth century quarry was so hard to find that many staghunts were forced either to disband or convert into foxhunts.

Another way the shortage of deer could be overcome was by hunting carted deer. Special deer were kept in captivity and one would be taken to unknown country on the day of the hunt, released and pursued until it had tired. Then it would be caught and returned unharmed to its home park. Often up to 20 miles (32km) would be covered in pursuit. King George III was one of the first to promote this form of hunting at the beginning of the nineteenth century. The sport caught on, particularly in South-East England, where a number of packs pursued carted deer: the Earl of Derby, for instance, kept a pack near Croydon. Today all of the British packs have been disbanded, the last – the Norwich – going in 1964, but in Ireland, the most famous hunting country in the world, the sport is still practised: by the Ward Union in the Irish Irish Republic and the County Down in Northern Ireland.

The sport of hunting wild deer still has many protagonists, especially in France where there are about 20 packs. There it is a tradition-bound form of hunting with hunt staff wearing the old elaborate, colourful liveries and using the melodic French hunting horn to relay information across the forests. Britain's only staghunting country is rugged, trappy Exmoor. In this beautiful open country there are few fences to jump, but numerous hills and much rough terrain to cross – a sure-footed, sturdy horse or pony is needed. A variation of staghunting, called buckhunting, is practised in the New Forest. In this form the quarry is the smaller fallow deer.

Below: George Stubbs' picture portrays the end of a staghunt – a form of hunting popular for many centuries but now rare except in France and a few areas of Britain. (*Cooper-Bridgeman*)

Right: Ladies always used to hunt side-saddle, like this lady in the Genessee Valley, New York State in 1892. (*Peter Newark's Western Americana*)

The staghunting season in England is longer than that for other forms of hunting. Stags are hunted in late summer, autumn and spring, and hinds in mid-winter. More ardent hunting folk in England take to hunting the stag in spring when the season for foxhunting – the most exciting form of hunting – is over.

It is likely that the fox and hare were hunted by country folk long before the aristocracy took to the sport. As deer became scarcer in their natural habitat, noblemen like the Duke of Beaufort started chasing foxes instead. The first hunt to concentrate on the fox was the Charlton in West Sussex, and foxhunting became a fashionable activity in the early eighteenth century. It was still a pretty slow form of hunting, for the ground tended to be heavy, the hounds rather large, and there were few fences.

Foxhunting in its modern form was developed mainly by Hugo Meynell, who was Master from 1753 to 1800 of what became Britain's premier foxhunt, the Quorn. During this period, more and more of the countryside was converted to grasslands divided by hedges in accordance with the Enclosure Acts and for the first time followers of the hunt had to jump to stay with the hounds. It added a new dimension of excitement which was taken even further by Meynell breeding faster

hounds. Other hunts followed the Quorn's example by breeding faster hounds and making it possible for followers to jump fences in the pursuit. The nineteenth and early twentieth centuries were a great time for the foxhunters. The countryside was ideal for running a good hunt and many of the participants were clever and rich men who dedicated their lives to the sport and to breeding and training better and faster hounds.

Today, wire fences and ploughed fields have made the countryside less easy and not so much fun for followers to ride across; motorways and urban developments have encroached upon and cut up the land: it is now difficult to run a good hunt. The quality of the sport has deteriorated; nevertheless this deterioration has had little affect on its popularity, for 250 hunts still prosper in Britain and in America new ones are being formed to add to the present total of about 140.

Foxhunting country in the British Isles varies enormously: from the hilly, trappy country in Wales, where Cobs are the most suitable mounts, to the undulating grasslands of the Shires, where a Thoroughbred is best for following hounds, to the small, green fields of Ireland divided by those huge, difficult banks that only a clever horse and a brave or foolhardy rider takes on.

In America there are equally great variations in country and climate. Hunting is carried on in the south in Georgia, where frosts rarely occur and the temperature can rise to 90 degrees in the hunting season. The most fashionable packs are found in Virginia and Maryland, and in the Piedmont region of Virginia there are eleven packs within a fifty-mile radius. Further north in New York, most of the hunts close down in January when the snow and ice gets the better of even the most ardent followers. For nearly all these areas the predominant jump is the 'chicken coop' – a sloping panel which was originally used to cover the wire. In Piedmont, Orange County, and Middleburg, however, there are stone walls, posts and rails which contribute to make these areas particularly popular.

Above: Hunting is not confined to the colder regions as proved by this American rider from the South. (*Peter Newark's Western Americana*)

105

Above: A day's foxhunting starts with the meet – an opportunity for riders and followers to talk and for the secretary of the hunt to collect the dues. (*Sylvester Jacobs*)

Foxhunting is practised in Australia too, although the shortage of foxes can force some packs to turn occasionally to hunting wallabies or even kangaroo, or to draghunting.

In Europe there is little foxhunting: just one pack outside Rome in Italy and another close to Lisbon in Portugal. The threat of rabies and the urbanization of the country has led to the sport being abandoned, largely in favour of draghunting.

The origins of draghunting can be traced to a sport promoted by the Stuart Kings called 'trail scenting' (hound racing). Supporters of the various canine competitors found that the best way of viewing their dogs was on horseback and that the chase itself was great fun. It took some time for this to develop into formal draghunting, when a scent is laid over prepared country, the hounds give tongue and the riders follow, taking on obstacles which vary in size and difficulty from pack to pack. During the nineteenth century Britain's youth at universities and in the Army took to draghunting when they discovered that this was a way of jumping the maximum number of fences in the shortest possible time.

Oxford University is thought to be the first to have organized a regular draghunt. Cambridge soon followed suit, as did some sections of the Army: the Household Brigade, the Royal Artillery and the Staff College.

Today's draghunting packs in Britain are civilian-run, except for the Staff College which still flourishes. They have been started in country where motorways and wire prevent the followers of foxhunting from getting much jumping. Draghunting is even more popular in Europe. In some countries such as Sweden, Denmark, Austria and Switzerland, it is the only form of hunting practised.

The principle of draghunting is for a line of anything from seven to fifteen miles to be organized, so that mounted followers can take on prepared obstacles when they pursue the draghounds. On the day of the hunt linemen, who can be mounted or on foot, pull a 'drag' across the

country. The 'drag' contains a scent which the hounds will want to follow when their huntsmen and whippers-in bring them to the beginning of the line.

The success of the venture depends on the hound having a good nose, drive and stamina, being able to run fast enough to give the riders some gallops – not so fast, however, that they leave the horses behind. The most important factor is the scent, for it has to appeal to the hounds and last long enough not to evaporate before the hounds are put on to it. A dampened ferret's nest was an early favourite, but the current fashionable 'drag' is either fox's urine/litter plus aniseed to prevent evaporation, or an artificial scent which has been developed by one of Britain's leading chemical firms.

As it is easier to pick up the scent of a 'drag', fewer hounds are needed, and five to fifteen couples (hounds are always counted in pairs) are usual. For a foxhunt, however, a large kennel might house as many as fifty to sixty couples, although less than a third of these would be used on a particular day's hunting.

A meet at any of these variations of hunting is a colourful occasion. The hunt servants will be in hunt coats. In charge is the Master, or sometimes Joint Masters, and they are responsible for the finances of the hunt. In the past this usually meant putting a good deal of money into the hunt's coffers for the privilege of acting as Master. The Master(s) also have the delicate and demanding job of getting permission from the farmers to hunt over their lands, and on the hunting day one Master usually acts as 'Field Master', which gives him the difficult task of leading and controlling all the followers. To do this well he has to be a bold man across country and a strong disciplinarian in order to control all the eager followers who want to be part of the action.

The Secretary is the administrator who does all the hunt's paperwork and collects the dues. These consist of subscriptions from members and 'caps', a fee paid by non-members for the privilege of a day's hunting.

At the meet the Huntsman is usually quiet, and merely keeps an eye on the hounds which he will be in charge of. He is probably the most important man with those eager for sport, as he works the hounds and helps them to find the fox. He is helped by the whippers-in, but it is the Huntsman who is the director.

Excitement begins to mount when the hounds move off to go to the first covert (an enclosure of trees, bushes or scrub). When they reach it, the hounds are put in and encouraged to work by the Huntsman, and the whippers-in are posted at strategic points to see if a fox breaks covert. If a hound finds a scent he will 'speak' and this encourages the rest of the pack to come to him and take up the scent. If it is a large covert the quarry may run around inside, but he will usually head off into the open. A whipper-in or follower will notice this, and as soon as the quarry is far enough away not to be frightened back into the covert, will cry 'View Halloa', and the Huntsman will blow 'Gone Away' on his horn.

To anyone who has caught the passion of foxhunting, this is a spine-quivering moment. A decision has to be taken quickly – to follow the Field Master or to risk everything and go one's own way. Usually there is only a second or two to think of what lies ahead – whether it will lead to a great chase, a fall, an injury, some huge fences, or merely a check and the loss of the fox. It is this excitement of tackling the unknown, the satisfaction that in the heat of the moment more courage can be built up than is ever normally possible, and the fascination of seeing animal nature at work, the hounds' techniques in picking up the scent, that makes hunting, however illogical, a sport which gives its many followers some of the greatest thrills and satisfaction of their lives.

Polo

Polo goes back as a sport almost as far in history as hunting. Its origins as a ball game on horseback are lost in antiquity. There are references to such a game in the time of Alexander The Great, but the original players are thought to have been Persians, for there is a manuscript dated about 600BC describing a match between the Persians and Turkomans. The Persians continued to practise the game well into modern times, for there are sixteenth-century paintings of teams of rather aristocratic gentlemen – and even ladies – hitting a ball from horseback.

The game of polo spread east, for it is known that the Chinese, Japanese and, in particular, the Mongolians were enthusiasts. Chinese and Moslem invaders took the game into India and it was there in the 1850s, in Assam, that some British planters first took note of the game and tried it out for themselves, setting up clubs and drawing up rules.

Those original British players rode the little 12.2hh Manipuri ponies and there were nine players to a team. When the game was taken to England larger, faster ponies were used and the team was reduced to four. Today, the ideal height for a polo pony is around 15.1hh.

The first recorded game in Britain was between the officers of the Life Guards and Royal Horse Guards in 1869, on Hounslow Heath near London. It was a success and thereafter the game was promoted by the Army in particular. Hurlingham became the headquarters and the

Right: Polo was originally practised mostly in the East. This Chinese Watercolour on silk dates back to the thirteenth century. (*Victoria & Albert Museum*)

Below, right: Only tough ponies and riders survive and enjoy the fast moving game of polo. The pony in the foreground is being turned very quickly so that his rider can pursue the ball. (*Sally Anne Thompson*)

Above: A lone polo player ahead of his team members and opposition swings the stick to hit the ball at Cirencester Park, Gloucestershire, England. (*Sally Anne Thompson*)

Hurlingham Polo Association was formed which drew up rules in 1875. Although the Hurlingham Ground is now covered with buildings and other sports facilities, British polo is still ruled by the same Association.

Polo was taken across the Atlantic soon after its establishment in Britain, and in 1885 the first international match was played between Britain and the USA. The Westchester Cup was at stake, and nine further series were staged for this trophy, the last being in 1936.

During the inter-war years international polo was played on the London Polo Grounds of Ranelagh, Roehampton and Hurlingham. It was a stimulating time for British polo, with regular visits of teams from India, Australia, the USA and the Argentine.

Major changes took place after World War II. The London Polo Grounds were built on and the war took toll of the administrators and players so that little polo could be played in Britain. Indian polo suffered even more, and, although the game still prospered in America, the title of leading polo nation was taken over by the Argentinians.

In Argentina excellent, athletic ponies were bred cheaply from Criollo stock. The land was flat and ideal for polo grounds, so that most *estancias* (Argentinian farms) laid out one or even two and ran strings of polo ponies. Polo grounds became almost as common as football grounds, with the result that there are five times as many players registered in Argentina as in the USA, and ten times more players than in Britain.

Argentina might be top of the polo league, but the USA is able to give them some competitions. The handicap of hard winters in the north has been overcome there by organizing arena polo. When the grasslands are frozen over or waterlogged ardent polo players switch their game to an area one third of the size of the summer version. Many of these arenas are indoors, although outdoor all-weather artificial surfaces may be used. In the smaller space only three players form a team and they use a leather covered ball (six inches in diameter). As this does not run as easily as the smaller willow ball arena polo is a slower game which is fun to watch and helps the Americans to keep their hand in during the bad weather.

In Britain, with no arena polo, the season is very short, running from late April to August. The game has, however, played an important part in British equestrian activities since its recovery from the post-war doldrums in the 1950s. This revival was largely due to Lord Cowdray who organized a club and its grounds on his Estate in Sussex, and to HRH Duke of Edinburgh and later, Prince Charles, who gave the game the stimulus of Royal patronage. Then, in the 1960s, a major step forward was made when the Pony Club added polo to their curriculum. This provided a new source of players and many graduated to become the mainstays of today's British game.

Australia and New Zealand are also great players of the game. In Australia the game can be played all year round: there is a winter season in New South Wales and a summer season in South Australia and Victoria. The major Australasian tournament is the Gold Cup played between Australia and New Zealand. It is very competitive with the smaller country emerging victorious almost as often as Australia.

Polo is a very invigorating game to play – galloping up and down that huge area (300 yards × 160 yards/274m × 146m), turning quickly on those agile little polo ponies, trying to mark opponents, and striving for the occasional satisfaction of hitting the tiny (two-inch/5cm diameter) willow ball hard and square. The speed of the game makes it potentially very dangerous, and collisions and spills would be frequent occurrences if players were allowed to play as they pleased. Strict rules are therefore enforced, reducing but not preventing accidents, and they sometimes make the game a little confusing to the spectator.

The two umpires who monitor the game on ponies will often blow their whistles for no apparent reason to the lay spectator. The usual reason is that one player has not observed another's right of way, which is given to the player following the line of the ball. Any opponent crossing the line once a player has acquired it is penalized.

Polo is, however, a pretty rough game for a player can 'ride off' his opponent. This happens when two opponents galloping alongside each other are both after the ball. They are allowed to bump and push until the stronger man and pony push the weaker pair off the line of the ball. It is also possible, when an opponent is about to hit the ball, to hook his stick. These rather ungallant tactics have nevertheless not prevented quite a number of girls from making their mark on the sport.

Galloping so fast and having to turn so quickly puts an enormous strain on the ponies, so they only play for a limited period of 7 minutes, which is known as a chukker (derived from the Indian word 'chakkar' meaning a circuit). A match lasts for 4, 6, or, very occasionally, 8 chukkers and there is always a half-time in the middle.

The speed and standard of the game will depend on whether it is a low, medium or high goal match. A high goal match is the most exhilarating to play and to watch, for it consists of players with the highest handicaps, i.e. the best. Each player is awarded a handicap of

Above: A F Tschiffely became famous after his marathon ride across South and North America. Here he is being congratulated by the mayor of San Antonio, Texas, in 1928. His adventure sowed the seeds for the development of long distance riding. (*Peter Newark's Western Americana*)

between −2 and + 10 goals, the former for the absolute beginners and the latter for the brilliant. There are only a handful of 10-goal players in the world, none at all in the UK, one in Australia, the odd one in the USA, but the majority in Argentina.

Before a match each team adds up the handicaps of its players and any difference between these totals is multiplied by the number of chukkers to be played and divided by six (the number of chukkers on which each player's handicap is based). This sum is then put as a score on the board against the team with the lower handicapped players. It thus becomes more competitive (like strokes in golf): the poorer team will have some goals to its credit before any player comes on to the field.

One other point that spectators should appreciate in order to enjoy the game, is that each time a goal is scored the teams change ends. With the high number of goals often scored in polo games it is very easy to miss a score and to then start yelling for your team to go the wrong way!

Spectators of polo have to concentrate to really enjoy the game; players need to be courageous, have a good eye for a ball, be good team members and, probably least important, to be able to ride. Great horsemanship is not needed to control these fleet footed, agile ponies in one of the most exhilarating of the equestrian sports.

Trail riding

Even less horsemanship is needed for trail riding, in which comparatively novice riders can enjoy crossing natural countryside on horseback. It has become a popular form of holiday to go trekking or to embark on pack rides in particularly beautiful parts of the world. Sometimes packs are taken not just for midday meals, but with equipment to camp out overnight or stay at a shack.

This rather leisurely form of riding has developed a more competitive side when speed and stamina are tested. This is known as 'distance

riding'. In Britain this takes the form of team relays over distances of ten to twenty miles, or more serious individual rides of about forty miles, and the ultimate is the annual Golden Horseshoe Ride of seventy-five miles over the picturesque, but wild land of Exmoor National Park.

This Golden Horseshoe ride is not a race, but standards are set and a competitor can lose marks if his horse's condition deteriorates, or if he does not complete the course at the required speed. Those without penalties receive Gold and those not quite so good, Silver or Bronze.

The key factor in these long distance races is the condition of the horse and rider. With thoughtful and thorough preparation, practically any type of horse and rider can do well, hence the attraction for so many people. The Arab horse, however, finds the stamina aspect much easier than other breeds. So although many native breeds are used, especially on the less demanding rides, in the ultimate tests it is the Arab or crossbreds with Arab blood that excel.

In the USA the sport takes a different form. Competitive rides are popular when contestants cover a specified distance within a stipulated time. Early or late arrivals are penalized. Then there is the more exciting endurance ride which is a race. The winner is the first to the finish, although a prize or prizes are given to the horses finishing in the best condition. Distances in both forms of distance riding vary from twenty to several hundred miles, and the event might take several hours or as much as a week.

Trail riding is a fast expanding sport with more than 500 distance rides in the United States and Canada. All over the world, however, the sport's expansion is being monitored by the veterinarians. With such a demand put on stamina and endurance there is a danger that ignorant or ruthless riders could ask too much of their horses. To prevent this, all competitions organize veterinary checks at regular intervals, when competitors in a bad state can be eliminated and the unsatisfactory acquire penalty points.

Above, centre: Trail riding in the US is a popular means of viewing such beautiful areas as the Rocky mountains of Colorado. (*Peter Newark's Western Americana*)

Above: Tourists in France can also trek across such picturesque areas as this Cirque de Gavarnie in the Pyrenees. (*J M Stewart*)

Distance riding is fulfilling an important rôle in the equestrian world. It encourages riders to become better horsemasters, to pay attention to the condition of their horse, and it provides an opportunity for the horses and riders who lack experience and brilliance to take part in a sport.

Driving

Horse driven carriages were the main means of transportation until the advent of the speedier motor car. After this the use of the driving horse for practical purposes almost faded into oblivion, but since the 1950s thousands of people have rediscovered the pleasure and exhilaration of travelling in a horse-drawn carriage.

There are three types of driving which are practised competitively. Coaching has the greatest connections with the past for teams of four or more horses pull historical coaches full of people on a marathon drive, and are judged both on the quality of the turn out and the fitness of the horses. Showing, which is also known as 'private driving' entails showing off the horse's paces and behaviour in an arena and being judged for this and general turnout. The third is combined driving, which is an exciting new competition – a three-day event on wheels when horses pull their carriages through dressage tests, across country and around an obstacle course in an arena.

Coaching is an expensive form of driving, for huge old coaches have to be kept in working order, grooms have to be hired and equipped with old-fashioned livery and matching horses have to be found and trained. Consequently many of the coaches are commercial ventures used as a means of advertising, as they are eye-catching on their drives down the road in marathons and general exercise, and they feature at major shows where many spectators take a great interest in these symbols of a bygone era.

Private driving is a very popular form of driving for the only vital requirements are a pretty pony or horse with good movement and a beautifully turned out carriage with gleaming brass, new paint and immaculately cleaned harness. The expense is not too great and any sensible person can, with a little effort, achieve this and the ability to drive a single or pair of horses or ponies around an arena. It is one equestrian form where the professionals have little advantage.

Combined driving is the most exciting and demanding form of competitive driving. The rules were only drawn up in 1969 and the first international contest was held in 1970 at Royal Windsor in the UK. International competitions are restricted to teams (four) or pairs of horses, but at national events there are sections for everybody – pony and horse singles, pony and horse pairs, pony and horse teams and even tandems when the two horses or ponies pull the carriage one behind the other, rather than side by side.

The first phase of combined driving is the dressage and some of the marks in this are given for presentation, i.e. the cleanliness of the carriage, the horse's condition, the driver's and groom's correctness and general smartness. After this inspection the contestants perform a set series of movements in an arena 330ft × 197ft (100m × 60m) and in the most difficult tests they have to collect and extend their trot and walk, rein back, and loop off and on to the track with the reins in one hand.

115

These movements become increasingly difficult the more horses or ponies there are to control. It takes great skill to get four powerful horses moving in harmony, stopping together, and then taking the same sized strides when they move into the trot.

The second phase – the marathon – is like the second phase in a three-day event, the one the competitors love, for there are many thrills involved. The crowd too, enjoy the spectacle of horses and carriage manoeuvring, and sometimes overturning, through difficult obstacles, between trees and into water. All of it has to be done at speed, for time is vital. On all sections of a marathon, which can be about eighteen miles, there are bogey times and penalties are incurred by those who are too slow or too fast.

There are walk sections and steady trot sections and one very fast section which includes all those tricky hazards. The hazards are marked slightly differently for they are surrounded by a penalty zone and it is only within this zone that the horses and ponies are allowed to break out of a trot into a canter. They have to get through the obstacle within the time allowed and must do this without the groom or driver getting on to the ground to assist the horses, otherwise penalties are given. For successful negotiation it takes a great understanding between the driver (known as a whip) and his horses. The whip must

Below: This is the third and final phase of Combined Driving. HRH Prince Philip is taking his team through an obstacle in the arena below Windsor Castle. (*Jane Kidd*)

anticipate and prepare for the problems and react quickly when difficulties arise; the horses must have courage, be obedient and brave.

After the gruelling test of a long marathon, contestants have to turn out on the next day for the final obstacle phase. In this a course is laid out in an arena. Each obstacle consists of two synthetic cones with rubber balls on their tops placed the width of the carriage wheels apart, plus 15 inches (39cm). The whip has to manoeuvre his horses and carriage through these obstacles without hitting a cone, which will dislodge a ball and incur a penalty.

The winner of a combined driving event is the contestant who has incurred the fewest penalties in all three phases. Internationally the most common victors are the Hungarians, although the Swiss, Germans and British win their share of medals at the European and World Championships.

In other countries it is a fast growing sport, particularly in the USA which is beginning to send teams abroad. Probably though, the greatest contributor to the sport has been HRH Duke of Edinburgh who, as President of the International Equestrian Organisation (F.E.I.), promoted the sport's creation, and as a leading competitor in Britain he has a popular supporter in the Queen, whose frequent attendance has given the sport even greater spectator appeal.

Below, left: Hungary produces the most successful drivers and driving horses in the world. These carriages are parading at one of the country's state studs of Bábolna. (*L Kacsor, Robert Harding Associates*)

Below, right: In the marathon phase of Combined Driving, competitors have to go through hazards which usually include a deep water like this one. (*Jane Kidd*)

117

The Olympic Competitions

The Olympics are the ultimate for any sportsman, and for the horseman there are three fields for which he can aim – show jumping, dressage or three day eventing. In the Greek Olympics (680BC–AD394) the equestrian sports were more tests of courage than skill, consisting as they did of chariot races and bare-back races. The modern Olympics were restarted in 1896 after a lapse of more than 1500 years. They were run under the principle that 'The main thing is not winning, but taking part, for the essential thing in life is not so much conquering as fighting well': worth noting when faced with today's growing professionalism.

Equestrian games did not feature in 1896 and were little more than side-shows at the 1900 Games, consisting merely of dressage, high jumping and long jumping. It was only after considerable negotiation that three Olympic Games later, at Stockholm, full-scale equestrian events were organized. The competitions were designed for the military who dominated horse sports of that period. There was a new type of competition – the Complete Test of Equitation – which lasted over four days and started with a thirty-four mile (55km) ride including a three-

Above: The most famous show jumping combination of all time, Harry Llewellyn and Foxhunter who between 1947 and 1955 won a record number of international classes and led the UK to victory at the 1952 Olympics. (*Desmond O'Neill*)

Left: A Tersky horse jumping in the USSR. The Russians take part but have never been as successful in show jumping as dressage. (*Sally Anne Thompson*)

Right: Marion Mould on her pony Stroller who consistently beat all the larger horses to win such events as a Ladies World Championship and an individual Olympic Silver medal. (*London Express News and Feature Service*)

mile (4.8km) cross country course, followed on the next three days by a two-mile (3.2km) steeplechase, show jumping and dressage. This was the forerunner of the three-day event.

Show jumping as a sport was also in its early stages, having progressed from 'leaping contests', which were first staged in Dublin over single fences forty-eight years before, to a simple course of fences in which the jumps were pretty low by today's standards. The maximum was 4ft 6in (1.4m) and some were only 3ft 3in (1m). At a modern Olympics no fences would be under 4ft 6in (1.4m).

Dressage had a long history as an entertainment if not as a sport, but the first Olympic competitions in this discipline seem to have been more of a test of obedience than gymnastic brilliance. The difficult movements – *piaffe*, *passage* and *pirouette* – were not included; just *flying changes*, *extended* and *collected paces*. However, five small fences had to be jumped and there was a special obedience test consisting in the main of passing by objects which made most horses shy.

Other forms of equestrian sports were tried at the Olympic Games – polo in 1908, 1920, 1924 and 1936, and vaulting in 1920; but only show jumping, dressage and three-day eventing have stood the test of time to become established as Olympic equestrian sports.

Show jumping

The most glamorous of these three sports in terms of its public following, prestigious prizes and promise of financial rewards is show jumping. In most countries it rates second only to football and athletics

Right: The American
international show jumper,
Neil Shapiro, riding Sloopy
at Germany's premier show,
Aachen. (*London Express
News & Feature Service*)

as a spectator sport. More than 880 million people all over the world watched on their televisions the ultimate competition – the team jumping at the 1976 Montreal Olympics. With this sort of public following, the prize-winners soon earn public renown and riders like Harvey Smith, Alwin Schockemöhle, D'Oriola, the D'Inzeo brothers, Bill Steinkraus and David Broome are household names. The enormous popularity of the sport also means that sponsors are eager to supply funds which will earn goodwill and publicity. The result is that the prize money is soaring, with a first prize of £3000 ($6000) now being quite commonplace.

Show jumping's popularity stems largely from the simplicity of the rules which makes the sport immediately understandable and exciting to even the most ignorant spectator. For the regular supporter there is the added attraction of the personalities involved – both of the riders and the horses. Television brings out the elegance of a horse like Philco, the power of the German-bred Gladstone, the audacious rough humour of farmer Ted Edgar, the intelligence of Alwin Schockemöhle, and the eagerness of Harvey Smith to shock the 'establishment'. The colourful, simple formula of show jumping has made it one of the most popular sports in the world.

International show jumping is ruled by the Fédération Equestre Internationale (F.E.I.), which has more than forty member countries. It defines a jumping competition as 'one in which the pair, competitor and horse, is tested under various conditions over a course of obstacles. It is a test intended to demonstrate the horse's freedom, its energy, its skill and its obedience in jumping, and the competitor's horsemanship.'

A competitor is penalized for making certain mistakes: knocking down an obstacle – 4 faults; refusing to jump or a disobedience the first occasion in a round – 3 faults, the second – 6 faults and the third – elimination; and the fall of horse or rider – 8 faults. The winner is the competitor who, by incurring least penalties, jumps the course in the fastest time or has the highest number of points, depending on the type of competition.

There is a great variety of competitions but the most common is the Table A class in which competitors with clear rounds go forward to a

Left: The 1976 individual Olympic champion from Germany, Alwin Schockemöhle does not always clear the fences. On this occasion he has met a serious problem at Hickstead's water ditch. (*Keystone*)

jump-off over a shortened course. In this round or in a second jump-off if the leaders have equal faults or clear rounds then the competitor with the fastest round is the winner; i.e. the first or second jump-off is 'against the clock'. This speed element is one of the most exciting aspects of show jumping but it is relatively new. The original concept was merely to clear the fences.

Before the last war and at national post-war shows the fences were difficult to clear for they were rather flimsy and easily knocked down. The emphasis was on precision – the rider could take his time to place his horse on exactly the right take-off point and the horse had to jump very carefully. If such fences were taken at speed – when horses tend to flatten in the jump and brush the fence – these light poles would fall to the ground; clear rounds could only be achieved at a very slow pace.

Today the fences are formidable, the poles do not fall so easily, the spreads are enormous and the horse needs great power and courage to jump them. Not only do they have to clear them but in order to win they

121

have to turn into the fence within a few strides to save those precious seconds. As a result a good show jumper now has to be well-trained on the flat so that he can maintain his balance and his power to spring into the air when turning sharply into a fence; he has to have enormous scope to jump high and wide over those massive obstacles; and he has to be very brave to do all this. Today's show jumper is very different from the cob-like horse of bygone eras which excelled over high, flimsy single fences but would not have the courage, scope or training for today's demands.

This training is needed not only to cut corners against the clock but to master another relative innovation in show jumping – related distances. Fences are now placed close to one another so that the horse has only a few strides between them. The course designer can set this distance so that the average horse can take his normal stride and arrive at a good place to take off for the next fence. On the other hand an additional test might be introduced; the distance set is such that if the horse takes his normal length of stride he arrives in a disastrous place to take off, far too close or too far back from the fence. The rider therefore has to decide whether to make his horse extend his strides or shorten them in order to get into a good take-off position. It is an excellent test of the obedience and training of the horse to see whether he will respond to his rider's demands, and of the horsemanship of the rider to be able to convey his wishes to his horse.

The obstacles themselves can be divided into two basic types – the upright and the spread. The upright can be a gate, a brush with poles above it, planks, or poles on top of one another. Uprights are rarely imposing-looking obstacles so the horse does not try so hard when jumping them. Therefore when the rider approaches them he has to collect his horse (shorten his stride and build up the power to spring into the air), judge accurately the correct place for take-off (further back than from a spread) to make it as easy as possible for the horse to clear the height.

Spreads involve jumping width as well as height and the most common types are the triple bar (a staircase fence) and the parallel

bars which are two sets of upright poles built parallel to one another with a spread between them of 3ft to 6ft 6in (0.9m–2m). The impressive appearance of a spread makes a horse more careful, but he will need much greater impulsion to jump width as well as height. The rider's aim is to approach spreads with more speed and to take off closer than to an upright in order to clear the spread.

An unusual form of spread is the water for this has great spread (10ft–17ft/3m–5m) but very little height; just a small brush on the take-off side. This demands a much more extreme version of the riding technique for spreads, as the horse must take off as close as possible to the water and with a good deal more speed than for any other obstacle.

In a Table A jump-off class there are approximately equal numbers of spreads and uprights, and a course designer usually alternates them so that competitors are tested further by constantly having to change technique – to ride on at the spread, land and steady the horse for the upright, and then ride on again for the next spread. There will be between ten and twenty fences in total, but some of these will consist of two (a double) or three (a treble) sections. There will be room for the horse to take only one or two strides between these sections; so it is good test of his boldness that he is willing to jump fences so close together, and of his balance that he can land and be able to take on another fence immediately.

Trebles and doubles, known as combination fences, play an important part in Table A jump-off classes but are rarely used in the various types of speed competition. These are the 'fun' classes to watch when the emphasis switches from jumping high fences clear to jumping lower ones at a great speed. Sometimes it is the fastest clear round which is the winner, but the most exciting are those in which competitors have seconds added to their total time if they hit a fence. This means that a competitor who hits a fence early on can risk all and by going flat out can make up the seven or ten seconds which were added to his total time.

There are also more unusual competitions like the Top Score when

Above: The practice jump. Robert, the brilliant son of the notorious Harvey Smith, starts over an obstacle just one-third of the size of those in the arena. (*Sylvester Jacobs*)

Above: Italy's Captain Raimondo D'Inzeo jumps a big wall. With his brother Piero he has been a mainstay of the Italian teams for thirty years. (*D O'Neill*)

Right: Chris Collins and Smokey bound into the dressage arena at the Kentucky World Three Day Event Championships. For a horse who is fit and eager for the cross country, it is difficult to remain calm in the dressage. (*Jane Kidd*)

each obstacle has the value of a specified number of points according to how difficult it is to jump. Each fence can be jumped twice and each time it is cleared the competitor is awarded the points due. The winner is the competitor with the highest number of points within the time allowed.

Then there is the Accumulator when there are progressively more difficult obstacles. One point is received for jumping the first, two for the second etc. The competitor with the highest number of points is the winner and if there is a tie then there is a jump-off against the clock.

There is one competition where time plays no part whatsoever, and that is the gruelling *puissance* or test. In this class a course of single high fences is shortened and raised in height in each jump-off (there are usually four jump-offs) until only one large spread and the great tall wall remain. At top level international shows the wall can go to 7ft (2.1m) or more with the powerful, brave German horses usually beating the more sensitive, speedy Thoroughbreds.

Show-jumping competitions are usually for individuals but there is an important international team competition known as the Nations' Cup (Prix des Nations). It is for teams of four riders from one country (although only the three best scores count), and each nation is entitled to hold just one Nations' Cup per year. The course is formidable for this is the major international team competition and its object is to compare the skill of riders and horses from different countries.

The leading contenders for these Nations' Cups – the top show-jumping countries – are USA, Germany and Britain. Usually one of these three wins the President's Cup – the international team championship awarded to the country which has collected the most points in Nations' Cups throughout the season. The countries who run them closest are Italy, France, Belgium and Ireland.

Eventing

Eventing is the pentathlon of the horse world – the all-round test of horse and rider. The horse must prove he is obedient, supple and balanced in the dressage; courageous, clever and fast in the cross country; and agile and careful in the show jumping. The rider must prove that he can teach a horse the required movements and ride him well enough to display them in the dressage arena; he must be brave and have a good sense of speed to ride across country; and he must have judgement and control in the show jumping. Eventing is a great challenge and one which more and more riders are taking up around the world.

There are three phases in every type of Event – dressage, cross country and show jumping. The contents and length of the cross-country phase vary, however, to make it more or less a test of stamina. It can be a relatively short section, in which stamina isn't really tested, and the event can be completed in one day – the One-Day Event. The cross-country phases can be extended to provide a slight test of endurance; then two days are needed – the Two-Day Event; and for the ultimate test, when only a fast horse with great stamina will excel, three or more days are needed – the Three-Day Event. This is such a test of the horse that two or three Three-Day Events per year is all that can be asked of the normal horse, whereas they can try a large number of

Above: Lucinda Prior Palmer, the great Three Day Event rider, who has twice been the individual European Champion and has won Badminton four times. (*Sally Anne Thompson*)

Above: A young competitor at an Event. Competitions are now staged for all ages and this youngster has just completed a cross country course. (*Sylvester Jacobs*)

One-Day Events and quite a few Two-Day Events.

The first stage of any Event is the dressage, which is difficult and sometimes hair-raising for the rider, who has to try and perform small circles, vary the length of strides from collected to extended trots and canters, ask his horse to go sideways, backward, halt at a particular point; all on a horse which is very fit, longing to gallop off across country and perhaps to give the odd buck just to show how well he is. It demands a great understanding between the horse and rider, many hours spent training beforehand to make the horse understand what is required of him and to rigorously gymnasticize him (make him supple, balanced and rhythmical in all the work).

The second phase, known officially as the speed and endurance phase, is the feature of any event. The dangers of jumping solid difficult obstacles at speed make it the most exhilarating phase for riders and the most spectacular for onlookers.

This phase varies in length, as does the size of the fences, according to the standard of the competition. The maximum distance is the 30km (18.6 miles) of the Olympics but is usually considerably less. It is divided into four sections; road and track, steeplechase, more road and track, and cross country.

The roads and tracks extend for miles – as much as 22.5km (14 miles), but it is the easiest part of the speed and endurance phase. The horse

Left: International British
rider Chris Collins sails
over a drop fence in the
cross country phase of an
Event. (*Sylvester Jacobs*)

has to complete it at 240m (262yds) per minute, which is a fast trot, but many riders walk sections or dismount to run beside the horse to give him a breather. They can canter later to make up the time. For a very fit horse it is quite relaxing to trot across country, but then the idea of the roads and tracks is to test whether the competitor is fit.

The roads and tracks are followed immediately by an exhausting test of speed and stamina – the steeplechase. This is especially difficult for it is a race against the clock rather than other horses, over racing fences. Contestants have to complete the 3–4km (2–2.5 miles) course at about 40 km.p.h. (25m.p.h.), which is close to flat out for all but the speediest Thoroughbreds. Horses that complete it without penalties are usually quite tired; nevertheless they have to set out again immediately on the second roads and tracks phase. This is when many of the riders allow their mounts to walk, or dismount to run alongside.

At the end of the second roads and tracks phase there is a compulsory ten-minute halt before the most fearsome test begins – the cross country. During this ten minutes of recuperation the horses are checked by a veterinary surgeon and every last-minute aid (washing the horse down, re-adjusting boots etc.) is employed by the riders, supporters and grooms. The cross-country phase is the one that really counts, and the horse needs every possible assistance.

Just before the end of the ten minutes the rider remounts and stands at the start to await his countdown. Only the foolhardy don't feel those shivers of tension and nervous anticipation, wondering how those hazards will ride, as the voice booms out 5, 4, 3, 2, 1, Off! Ahead lie up to forty obstacles stretched out over as much as 8km (5 miles). They may not be quite as high as show jumps – maximum dimensions in the ultimate test, the Olympics, being 1.2m (4ft) high and 1.8m (6ft) wide – but they are solid, unusual and sometimes terrifyingly tricky.

The huge, solid fences, parallel bars, hedges, sleeper tables etc. look horrifying to riders and spectators alike but most horses think nothing of them, taking them with one easy bound in their galloping stride. It is the 'problem' fences that, although they are rarely very large, are not straightforward and therefore test the agility and courage of the horse, and the skill of the rider much more than the big fences.

A problem can be caused because a fence is spooky. Most horses need plenty of practice over gaping, dark ditches, jumping into water or taking off into what appears to be a vacuum because there is a big drop on the landing side. Confidence is the vital factor over these obstacles. Once he has acquired it the horse will trust his rider, and however frightening it might appear just before taking off, will still do so without hesitation.

The real problems are caused by those tricky fences where not just courage and scope are tested, but nimbleness, cleverness and obedience. There might be a bounce fence when the horse has no room for a stride but lands and takes off again immediately for the next fence. There might be combinations with difficult distances or turns between them or a 'coffin'. The latter is simply a post and rails followed by a ditch and then another post and rails, but it usually causes lots of grief because the horse's attention is taken by the ditch so that he refuses or does not jump the first element correctly.

Then there are the natural fences which are typical of the country in which the Event is being held. They may consist of hedges, ditches, a water which has to be jumped over, not into, banks, stone walls, jumps into or among forests or groves of trees. The latter can be difficult because of the change of light. Horses are very suspicious of jumping into darkness from bright sunlight and vice versa.

The rider having walked the course once, twice or even three times, will have analyzed the best way to approach each fence. He will known when his horse will need extra speed to tackle the 'big ones', extra courage (given with a kick, a slap with the whip or the voice) for the spooky ones, and greater collection at an awkward combination or if the approach is on an angle. The key to successful cross-country riding is building up trust between horse and rider to the point at which the horse knows that his rider will never ask him to do the impossible.

The cross-country section is in all Events, although it varies from very short with small fences for children and riding clubs to long and unbelievably difficult for the Olympics. The other sections can be removed: in a One-Day Event there is no steeplechase or roads and tracks, and in a Two-Day Event just a short steeplechase and roads and tracks section. These easier versions are used to introduce young horses and inexperienced riders to Eventing. In these they can gain confidence and experience; but the majority of horses and riders never progress beyond this level. The demands of the Three-Day Event are so great that only the fittest partnerships can think of participating.

The final phase of the Event is the show jumping. It might seem mundane after the excitements of the cross country, especially as the fences are small in comparison to those taken on by show jumpers. But for the Eventer it is very difficult to get a horse to jump slowly and carefully after galloping boldly over fixed fences. It becomes a great test of suppleness and obedience for the horse, and of the coolness of the rider's nerves, for often a clear round is vital. Just one pole brushed off can change the placings. It happens all too often. In the 1976 and 1964 Olympics Karl Schultz and Richard Meade respectively were leading for the individual gold medal, but, because of careless jumping rounds, they both lost this, the greatest honour in the sport. The aim of Eventing is to test all-round ability: the top riders have to be masters of all three phases.

Above: Drop fences are a feature of most Event courses and this, the Normandy Bank at Badminton, is one which takes great courage to jump. (*Sally Anne Thompson*)

Dressage

Dressage is simply training the horse – not merely to be obedient, but to establish a harmony between horse and rider, so that the horse gives the impression of doing of his own accord whatever has been asked of him. A mental rapport is needed to establish a clear understanding between horse and rider, and one in which the horse works 'with', not 'for' his partner.

This mental rapport is also required to succeed in the physical demands of dressage; to turn the horse into a gymnast who is supple, elastic in his movements, has spring to his strides (known as cadence) and develops power like a coiled spring which the rider can contain in the *collected paces* and release in the *extended gaits*.

Right: The veterinary inspection at Badminton. After the rigours of the cross country at a Three Day Event all horses must be passed sound before being allowed to jump. (*Sylvester Jacobs*)

Riding a top-class dressage horse should be a little like tending a furnace – the more raw materials (training plus talent) put in the greater the power generated – but it has to be controlled and the more the rider dares the greater the risk of explosion. The rider is sitting on a powerhouse and skill in dressage lies in the ability to persuade the horse to perform the required movements spectacularly but without resisting the aids.

This absence of resistance (known as submission) is an important aspect of dressage. It is no use building up the power if this is at the cost of the horse's co-operation. Swishing tails, stiffness in the back or not accepting the bit (avoiding the rein aids by either sticking his head in the air or bending his neck so his head comes close to his chest) show a lack of harmony and are severely penalized. The rider has to ask as much as possible of his horse, without building up resistance.

In a dressage competition the rider performs a series of movements in an arena (20m × 60m/66ft × 197ft) for international events, (20m × 40m/ 66ft × 132ft for some national events). He is given marks from 0 (movement not executed) to 10 (excellent) by a judge or judges for each movement. His score is added up upon completion of the test and the competitor with the highest score is the winner.

Above: The outstanding Canadian dressage rider, Cindy Neal, practises *passage* in front of Goodwood house at Britain's international show. (*Sylvester Jacobs*)

Inevitably the scores given by different people judging the same test do vary because each mark is a matter of opinion. The judges have to evaluate the performance and whereas one might put a premium on accuracy another might forgive mistakes if the horse was very supple and keen to go forward. Dressage is the equestrian art form and, as for all arts, there is a divergence of opinion as to what is best.

Then there is an additional practical problem: when there are a number of judges they see the movement from different angles which will give different impressions. Dressage judges are therefore subject to the criticism that they cannot agree, but the varying appreciations do give the riders the opportunity to train the horse *their* way, to try and make him *their* art form, a means of expressing what *they* want of a horse. Thus some dressage horses are gay but mischievious, others might be obedient but a little sombre, some might be very supple but not always straight, and others accurate but a little stiff – the trained horse is a reflection both of his rider's ability and his character.

The dressage movements which are used to gymnasticize the horse, and in the competition to test his training have been devised over the ages. Firstly there are the variations within the paces themselves. The young horse is asked to perform only at a working trot, canter and a medium walk. But with training he will learn to vary the length of his strides and outline. From the working trot he will be asked for more collection which entails taking higher, shorter steps. The whole of his outline will be shortened with the hindquarters lowered, the hind legs coming further under his body and the neck coming higher with the head perpendicular to the poll.

Collecting must be a gradual process for it entails great suppleness and development of the muscles and it will only be after two or three years of training that a true collected walk, trot and canter can be performed. With collection comes greater ease of carriage so that the horse becomes a more pleasureable ride – lighter and more mobile in his forehand and with great power being generated in his hindquarters.

Collecting the paces is alternated with extending them. The horse is

Above: One of the great dressage riders of the post war era – Josef Neckermann. He was a member of German gold medal teams in Olympic, World and European Championships and himself won individual honours. (*London Express News and Feature Service*)

gradually elasticized and power in the hindquarters developed so that he can take longer and longer steps, but without quickening, for that vital ingredient in dressage – rhythm – is always to be maintained. It is the extended paces which are the most invigorating to ride and the most spectacular to watch.

The horse must be taught to go backwards as well as forwards. He must learn to stand still with the legs forming four sides of a rectangle (known as a *square halt*). He has to turn on his hindlegs with the radius of the circle just his own length. This is known as a *pirouette*, and although relatively easy at the walk, needs great collection in the canter (it is not performed at the trot) if the horse is to retain his rhythm and perform it fluently.

At the canter the horse is normally expected to lead with the inside leg, but in the *counter canter* he has to lead with the outside leg, which is much more difficult. Changing the leading leg in the canter can be done through the trot or walk (known as a *simple change*) but the more advanced horses can remain in the canter while changing the lead. This is spectacular to watch, and difficult to perform when the lead is changed every fourth, third, second and eventually every stride.

Apart from going forwards, backwards and turning circles the dressage horse has to go sideways. In a number of what are called lateral movements the horse steps sideways as well as forwards. To do these well the horse must have a very supple back. There are a number of ways a horse can go sideways. In *shoulder-in* he brings his forehand in off the track so that he is slightly bent around the rider's inside leg, and his hind legs remain on the original track. In the *renvers* the forehand is brought off the track again but this time it is bent in the direc-

tion the horse is going. The *travers* is an inverted *renvers* for the forehand remains on the original track and the hindquarters are brought in. In the prettiest of these lateral movements – the *half pass* – the horse moves across an arena as close as possible parallel to the long side with both the front and hind legs crossing over.

Lateral work, extensions and collections and flying changes turn the dressage horse into a better and better gymnast until eventually (after three to four years of training) he is able to learn the most advanced movements in dressage competitions – the *piaffe* and *passage*. These are both very collected variations of the trot. In the *piaffe* the trot is performed on the spot and in *passage* the horse goes forward but the moment of suspension is prolonged, which makes it very elegant to watch.

Passage and *piaffe* are asked for in the Olympic test – the Grand Prix. Although the contents of the Grand Prix remain the same, the choreography – the sequence of these movements – is changed every four years, in pre-Olympic year. At the Games the Grand Prix decides the team championship but the 12 best-placed individual riders qualify for an even more difficult test – the Grand Prix Special or Ride Off Test. This short and exceptionally demanding test determines who the individual medallists will be.

In the three Olympic disciplines – show jumping, eventing and dressage – medals can be won in non-Olympic years, for the international ruling body (the F.E.I.) have devised championships – a World Championship, two years before the Olympics, European Championships in the years preceding and following the Olympics – and the international rider now has plenty of opportunities to prove his talents.

Above, centre: One of the prettiest combinations in international dressage, Irina Karacheva and Said complete a pirouette at the World Championships at Goodwood. (*Jane Kidd*)

Above, right: The European Dressage Championships at St Gall in Switzerland, with Britain's Diane Mason and Special Edition performing *passage*. (*Jane Kidd*)

133

The Racecourse

Horse racing is one of the world's most popular spectator sports, although for many people the attraction is not the excitement of seeing beautiful horses vying with each other at tremendous speeds, but the thrill of selecting a horse to win and betting on that judgement. The lure of betting and the large sums that may be involved have enforced a professional approach to the sport. Strict rules and regulations are needed to prevent malpractice and fraud; the big prizes, and the huge prices paid for horses likely to win prestigious and remunerative races has turned horse racing (in particular flat racing) into more of an industry than a pastime.

Flat racing

Horse racing has changed a great deal from the original concept which is thought to have been matches between only two horses. There are indications that races of this sort took place in Britain during the Roman occupation, but there is proof that a planned race was held between the horses of Richard II and the Earl Arundel in 1377. In the reign of James I the sport began to acquire a more organized approach. The King built a palace at Newmarket in Suffolk; he preferred hunting and breeding horses but encouraged his followers to go racing.

Newmarket developed into 'the' racing centre, a status it retains to the present day. Charles I was a keen follower of racing there, but it was Charles II who was the first ardent promoter of the sport. He even rode in matches and the Newmarket course – the Rowley Mile – was named after his favourite hack. He founded the Town Plate, and the condition that 'it should be run on the second Thursday in October for ever', has been complied with to this day.

The races held in the period following the Restoration were much longer than today's, ranging from 4 to 12 miles (6.5km to 19.3km), and the horses needed strength and stamina more than great speed. The original British racehorses were mainly ponies, known as Galloways (extinct since the last century), but faster Oriental stock began to be imported in the reign of James I, and arrived in even larger numbers during the subsequent reigns. Between 1660 and 1760 more than 200 Arabs, Turks and Barbs were brought to England and amongst these were three stallions to which all modern Thoroughbreds can be traced.

The earliest of the three vital imports was the Byerley Turk which was captured from the Turks in 1686 and later ridden by his new owner Captain Byerley at the Battle of Boyne. The second was the Darley Arabian which was foaled in 1700 and bought from Sheik Mirza by Thomas Darley. The third was the Godolphin Arabian, which was given to Louis XIV by the Emperor of Morocco and later sold to Edward Coke of Derbyshire.

Above: An exciting but less serious form of racing is 'skijoring' which on this occasion is being staged in Austria. (*Sally Anne Thompson*)

These three stallions were largely responsible for the greatly improved quality of the British racehorse by the middle of the eighteenth century. Associated with this improvement was such a surge in the popularity of the sport that it worried the government, and in 1740 a law was passed laying down standards and preventing too haphazard a multiplication of the sport by stating that no meeting could be held unless the plate was worth more than £50 (about $100).

This effort to regularize the sport was furthered by the formation of the Jockey Club in 1752, a body which gradually increased its influence until by the early nineteenth century it had established the role it plays today: acting as executive of racing, creator of rules, collector of fees and organizer of the training gallops at Newmarket.

The administration of the sport fell into the hands of the Weatherby family. It was they who in 1778 published the first Racing Calendar (listing runners, handicaps, forfeits etc.), and in 1791 started the General Stud Book – listing all Thoroughbred brood mares and stallions with their pedigrees. Today Weatherbys perform the same tasks but with the aid of computers and a large staff to deal with the increased volume of work.

In the middle of the eighteenth century the nature of racing began to change. Racing, which had begun as an extra test of stamina and strength for horses which were used in battle, to hunt or pull carriages,

135

Top: The race of the Palio – a race through the streets of Florence which was thought to date from the early fifteenth century. (*Cleveland Institute of Art*)

Above: Racing in the eighteenth century at Siena in Italy where they still race through the streets today. (*Robert Harding Associates*)

was becoming much more serious and specialized. The development of the Thoroughbred led to horses being used solely for racing, so the most spectacular element – speed – became more important than stamina or strength. The races were shortened, matches were replaced by races for a number of runners and younger horses were used.

Originally no horses under five years old were raced as they needed maturity to carry the heavy weights over the long distances of the early races. Then in 1756 a three-year-old race was run at Newmarket and in 1776 the first of today's most prestigious races – the Classics, which are confined to three-year-olds – was staged. It was a two-mile sweepstake for three-year-olds named after General Anthony St Leger which was run at Doncaster, and news of the success of the venture filtered south. Allegedly it was at the Oaks, an inn close to Epsom, that a race over 1½ miles (2.4km) for fillies was devised in 1778 and named after the inn. The first time the race was run in 1779 it proved to be a popular innovation so that in 1780 a counterpart for colts was inaugurated and named The Derby after Lord Derby, who was a frequent visitor to the Oaks.

To complete the Classic picture two more races for colts and fillies were devised over the shorter distance of 1 mile (1.6km). The Two Thousand Guineas for colts was first run at Newmarket in 1814 and the Thousand Guineas for fillies in 1819. The greatest achievement for any three-year-old colt or filly was, and still is, to win the Triple Crown – all three Classics – the 1 mile/1.6km (Guineas), the $1\frac{1}{2}$ mile/2.4km (Derby or Oaks) and the $1\frac{7}{8}$ mile/3km (St Leger). The first horse to win the Triple Crown was West Australian in 1853 and the last Nijinsky in 1970.

After the successful inauguration of the three-year-old race it was a natural progression to two-year-old races which enabled breeders to reap even quicker returns for their investments and more rapid proof of whether their mares and stallions were going to produce winners. This more commercial form of racing was tried in 1786 when a two-year-old race was run at Newmarket. The young Thoroughbreds were very fast but lacked stamina to run a long way, so the race distances were shortened still further to less than a mile.

By the middle of the nineteenth century today's format of racing had been established. There were 5–7 furlong races for two-year-olds and sprinters, $1-1\frac{3}{4}$ mile (1.6–2.8km) races, which included the Classics, and races over $1\frac{3}{4}$ miles/2.8km (but rarely more than $2\frac{1}{2}$ miles/4km) for the older horses, the stayers. Most of the flat racers' careers spanned the two- and three-year-old seasons. After this successful horses were rewarded with early retirement to stud, big slow horses usually started more dangerous careers racing over fences, and the smaller horses were exported to run in countries where the racing was less competitive.

The studs of the eighteenth century made Britain famous, for no other country was able to develop a horse as fast as the Thoroughbred. Consequently during the eighteenth and early nineteenth centuries British horses were exported to act as foundation stock for race horses in practically every country in the world. The British Thoroughbred became 'the' flat race horse the world over, although special restricted races were and are still staged for breeds such as Arabs in France, Eastern Europe and the Middle East, and for Quarter Horses in America.

Many of the early exports went to North America with the emigrants. The first recorded organized race in the USA was run on Long Island at the appropriately-named New Market in 1664. The instigator was the Governor of New York, Richard Nicolls. The sport flourished and has, in combination with harness racing, become the biggest spectator sport in the USA.

The sport started by being based on British principles with a Jockey Club being formed in 1790. Today there are major differences between the American and British Jockey Clubs. The American organization advises and runs stud books, colours etc., but state racing commissions have become the governing bodies for running and administering racing in individual states. Thus there is variety in this great country for although all states except New York prohibit off-track betting, some run pari-mutuels (totalizators) which make a major contribution to the state's funds, while others ban betting of any type and there are different rulings on permissible drugs from state to state.

Above: The flat race jockeys ride with much shorter stirrups than their counterparts who have to stay on over fences in steeplechases. (*Sylvester Jacobs*)

Right: A tight finish at Woodbine, the famous Canadian course. In Canada and North America the majority of races are run on 'dirt', rather than grass. (*Robert Estall*)

138

Left: The Parade ring at
Epsom on Derby day. HM
the Queen, an enthusiastic
owner of flat-race horses,
stands in the centre.
(*Spectrum*)

The result is that racing centres have developed in states which
promote racing and allow betting, and the most important are New
York, Chicago, Miami and Los Angeles; with New Jersey, Maryland,
Delaware, Massachusetts, Kentucky and New Mexico also organizing
important meetings.

The format of the meetings also differs from Britain's. The one to four
day meetings staged in the British Isles would not be feasible in the
USA where huge distances have to be covered. The result is that in the
USA a meeting normally runs for at least six weeks and the horses that
enter are trained at the track for its duration.

Classic races were not started until the late nineteenth century: the
Belmont in 1867, the Preakness in 1873 and the Kentucky Derby in
1875. These are run within a short period – less than two months – as
opposed to more than four in Britain. Distances run are also shorter:
the Preakness 9.5 furlongs, the Kentucky Derby 10 furlongs and the
Belmont 12 furlongs (cf. British classics which range from 8 to 15
furlongs).

Racing in Canada is not such a major industry as in the USA, and
many of the brilliant horses bred there (e.g. Northern Dancer) go south
to run. Most of the Canadian meetings are concentrated in Ontario
with the Woodbine track being the most popular.

The only country to rival the American and British standard of racing
is France, although the sport is expanding fast in Australia. France has
the great advantage that the majority of the money poured into betting
by the general public is directed into the sport rather than the government coffers or bookmakers' purses. The result is that France boasts
high prize money, magnificent racecourses and substantial aid for
breeders, all from money lost by bettors.

Right: The picturesque Chantilly racecourse. The surrounding area is the base for most of the important training stables in France. (*Sally Anne Thompson*)

Below, right: Flat races being over a shorter distance than steeplechases need a level start. It is normal to use starting gates like this one at the Piatigorsk course in the USSR. (*Sally Anne Thompson*)

With the disruptions of the Napoleonic wars the sport did not get under way until later than in Britain and America. Most of the imports of British Thoroughbreds took place in the 1820s and 1830s. The French Jockey Club was formed in 1833 and the Société d'Encouragement pour l'Amélioration des Races de Chevaux was formed one year later to act as the administrators.

The French Classic, the Prix du Jockey-Club, which was to become the equivalent of the British Derby, was first run in 1836. The Poule d'Essai des Poulains and the Poule d'Essai des Pouliches became the equivalent of the British Guineas, being run over the same distance – 8 furlongs – and at the same time of the year – late April or early May. The importance of a third, longer Classic was lost with the development of the most prestigious international race in the world – the Arc de Triomphe. Open to horses aged three and above, it has been run over 12 furlongs since its inauguration in 1920. It attracts the best horses in the world from Britain, Scandinavia, Russia, Italy, Germany and occasionally America. Its victors include such great champions as Ribot, Sea Bird, Vaguely Noble and Mill Reef, but it has seen the defeat

of such stars as Nijinsky and Troy. Probably the latter's hard summer campaigns had drained them of their drive by the time this race was run in October.

Australia's racing era began long ago for a meeting was held at Hyde Park, Sydney, in 1810 but it is only since the last war that standards and popularity have really boomed. There are now more than 700 tracks and 3500 racing days. Most of these tracks are oval with tight corners so that the spectators are rarely far from the action.

Although Classics are staged in each of the states, the most popular races are the handicaps. The Melbourne Cup, run on the first Tuesday in November, holds pride of place with the entire nation halting activities during its running.

Although racing is popular the world over it is the French, American and British-bred horses which dominate the international honours. The odd champion emerges from South America; Italy had a good spell when the brilliant breeder Frederico Tesio produced such great horses as Donatello, Nearco and Ribot, but no horses of this class have emerged since his death. Germany is improving her Thoroughbreds' standards which now earn occasional placings in big races and wins in the smaller ones. South Africa runs a thriving racing industry but her horses do not run internationally because of health restrictions; the existence of African Horse Sickness there has led to a ban on South African horses entering most countries. Japan and Hong Kong have made huge investments into bloodstock and have built impressive racecourses, but it is unlikely that their climates are suitable for the rearing of world-class racehorses.

All of these flat racing-orientated countries are continuously exporting and importing stock, and top-class jockeys are jet-setters with the likes of Lestor Piggot riding in at least a dozen countries each season. Flat racing has become big international business but the other forms of horse racing still remain more national affairs.

Steeplechasing

In steeplechasing the risk element of taking on fences in a race makes it spectacular for viewers, thrilling but dangerous for the jockeys, and a venture which owners join for love of the sport rather than the prospect of high commercial returns. Its appeal is limited to sporting people who enjoy risks and danger. There are enough supporters in the British Isles to make it almost as popular as flat racing, but nowhere else is steeplechasing as popular. In France and America huge prizes can be won but there are relatively few participants and meetings. In Germany, Belgium, South Africa, Australia and New Zealand it is staged as a more amateurish affair.

The sport started in Ireland when foxhunting gentlemen keen on sport, needing to prove their courage and the speed of their horses, challenged one another to race across country. The first recorded occasion was a match between O'Callaghan and Blake in 1752, when they raced from Buttevant Church to St Leger Church. The church steeple was their guide – hence the name steeplechase.

142

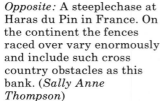

Opposite: A steeplechase at Haras du Pin in France. On the continent the fences raced over vary enormously and include such cross country obstacles as this bank. (*Sally Anne Thompson*)

Left, above: The huge chair fence on the Grand National Course claims many victims. This horse, Colleen Rhu, had a horrifying fall. (*Press Association*)

Left, below: Water jumps are part of most steeplechase courses, but this one is more difficult as there is no brush fence in front to encourage horses to take off. (*Jane Kidd*)

At first steeplechases were run across natural country. Then a course was prepared in Bedford in 1810, but the fences were so fearsome that only two participants could be mustered. Later efforts were less awe-inspiring and the sport flourished, with the most famous race in the world – the Grand National – starting in 1837. The fences at its Aintree course were and have remained the largest for any race in Britain, although today they are more straightforward than in early days. They are still 5ft (1.5m) or more high and the largest – the Chair – has the additional hazard of a 6ft (1.8m) ditch in front of it. The most famous fence is Becher's Brook because the huge drop on the landing side unbalances many runners and leads to numerous falls.

Other countries have tried to emulate the Grand National by building fearsome courses to race over, but none have succeeded in earning the same status. The Grand Pardubice in Czechoslavakia is more difficult for it contains the largest steeplechase fence in the world – the Taxis – which is a 5ft (1.5m) fence in front of a 16ft 5in (5m) ditch. Following this is such a variety of fences that few horses, sometimes not even the winner, complete the course without one or more falls.

143

Right: The largest steeplechase fence in the world – the Taxis at the Pardubice racecourse in Czechoslovakia. Few horses get over it without falling. (*Jane Kidd*)

Below, right: The Grand Pardubice race attracts spectators and entries from all over the world. Contestants need to be brave to take on such obstacles as this wide open water. (*Jane Kidd*)

However, tucked away behind the Iron Curtain it does not attract the publicity or the standard of horses of Britain's Grand National.

The Grand National is Britain's most famous race but it is the Cheltenham Festival meeting which attracts the highest calibre of horses as many owners do not wish to risk their horses over those fearsome Aintree fences. The Cheltenham fences are still big enough for at every British course they must be 4ft 6in (1.4m) or more and at Cheltenham they are made of tightly packed brush which does not yield and causes horses to fall when they hit it. In addition the course is on undulating ground with some of the fences on steep downhill slopes which only a balanced horse can jump. Thus out of the forty-four steeplechase tracks in Britain, Cheltenham with its testing conditions is considered the premier course.

At the Festival meeting in March the most important race is the Gold Cup. This is the premier race for the great horses of the era and the best of all its winners was Arkle who was victorious three times (1964, 1965 and 1966). He was owned by the Duchess of Westminster and trained in Ireland by Tom Dreaper. The only steeplechaser with comparable 'class'

was Golden Miller who won both the Gold Cup and the Grand National before the war.

Steeplechases only fill about half the race card at any British meeting for there are also races over lower fences known as hurdles. Standing just 3ft 6in (1m), these strongly-made versions of sheep hurdles have gorse laced between their rails. They were allegedly raced over by the British Prince Regent and his royal party in their hacks over the Brighton Downs in the early nineteenth century. After this they were incorporated into some of the steeplechase courses but eventually became a separate form of race.

Racing over hurdles puts a greater emphasis on speed than jumping ability. The stars are usually ex-flat racers for the larger, more sturdily-built steeplechasers are usually too slow. Hurdle races are, however, used as an introduction to racing for steeplechasers, enabling them to get the idea of racing with less likelihood of paying the painful penalty of inexperienced jumping – a fall.

The hurdlers' most prestigious race is, like the steeplechasers' Gold Cup, held at Cheltenham, at the Festival meeting. It is known as the

Above: A British steeplechase fence consisting of 4ft 6in (1.4m) high tightly packed brush. These runners are clearing it in fine style. (*Tony Boxall, Spectrum*)

145

Right: The finish of a hurdle race at Brussel's picturesque course, where there is an infinite variety of fences to be jumped. (*Jane Kidd*)

Champion Hurdle and its greatest heroes have been Persian War, Bula and Night Nurse.

The only other country to have anything like the same professional approach to racing over fences is France. In that country although the fences are often unusual they are not as high or stiff as the British versions and do not need such great jumping ability; so speed once again becomes vital. High-class flat-race horses take to racing over fences in France especially for the remunerative prizes given at the country's premier track, Auteuil, close to Paris.

Jump races are staged in Australia, South Africa, Belgium and Holland but the amateur is the mainstay of the sport. In America too the sport is dominated numerically by the amateur for few of the highly commercial major tracks run jump races, since they do not yield a high enough betting 'take'. Punters feel that the fences provide too great an element of luck and save their money for the horses which stay on the ground. American steeplechasing has thus become more of a spectacle than a betting medium which restricts its popularity. One steeplechase a day is wedged in between the ten or so flat races at some of the leading tracks during June, July and August. They race over plastic fences, the top of which can be brushed through, but the lower two-thirds is solid.

The hard core of American steeplechasing takes place at the Hunt meetings, one of which is run each weekend from March to May and again from September to November. The races are various, some over those plastic fences used at the major tracks, others with no fences at all, and some over timber. The timber consists of solid posts and rails which vary from 3ft (0.9m) for some easy courses to a terrifying 5ft (1.5m) for the famous four-mile Maryland course which is run over just once a year for the Maryland Hunt Cup.

International steeplechases started in the USA with the 1970 Colonial Cup in South Carolina. Runners enter this race from Australia, Ireland, Britain and France, but it was a number of years before the visitors beat their hosts, and the first to do so was the New Zealand-bred, British-trained Grand Canyon. In 1979 another steeplechase, the Hardscuffle, run in Kentucky, was added to the international calendar. It

seems the trend is towards the internationalization of steeplechasing but the attractions of such a move are very different from those of flat racing. There are none of the incentives of massive prize money, increasing breeding value: it is the excitement of something new, a different challenge which gets the sporting steeplechasing fraternity to try their hazardous sport in different countries.

Point-to-point

The amateur rider is a keen participator in all forms of jump racing, and in countries where steeplechasing has become too high-powered for the inexperienced jockey and for those who cannot devote much time to the sport, point-to-points were introduced. England and Ireland are the homes of this sporting form of jump racing which is confined to amateurs and to horses which have certificates to prove that they have been fairly hunted that winter. The season does not start until February to enable riders to give their mounts a good number of days in the hunting field; and it ends in May before the ground gets too hard to gallop over.

The fences can be 3in (75mm) smaller (4ft 3in/1.2m) than steeplechase

Above: A hurdle race at Plumpton which is one of the British racecourses. Hurdles being lower and not fixed cause fewer falls than steeplechase fences. (*Tony Boxall, Spectrum*)

Right: A training spin along the artificial gallop on top of the beautiful Downs in Sussex, England. (*Jane Kidd*)

versions and they are usually softer so that horses can brush through them without falling. They are simple brush fences except for the occasional one which has an open ditch in front of it. Only in Ireland do they have the odd race over banks. This is quite a change from the original point-to-point as it was in the last century. It was started as an informal race for foxhunters and was, as the name implies, a race across natural country from one point to another.

In America point-to-points are closer to those original versions. Although some are run over formal courses of brush fences many more are over timber and there are some flagged courses across natural country. The American season is shorter, from mid-February to mid-April, but the variety of races ensures that there is a version for even the most amateurish rider or the slowest horses as long as they can jump. Some of the more unusual races include owner-rider races, heavyweight races, junior flat races and hunting pairs; although most meetings include the more conventional maiden, ladies' and gentlemen's races.

In the British Isles, although the point-to-point is confined to the amateurs, it has become a more serious stereotyped occasion. The races are run over three miles or more and include an Open, a Ladies (point-to-points were the first form of racing to allow women to participate), some restricted races like a Members Race (confined to members of the hunt holding the point-to-point), Adjacent Hunts (confined to members of the surrounding hunts), and a Maiden (for horses which have not won).

Point-to-points are run by hunts, each holding one a season. These informal forms of jump racing are a major source of income to the hunts. The outlay is not too large, prize money is moderate in order to discourage professionalism, and the income is good for they are important local occasions drawing large numbers of spectators.

Harness racing

Harness racing has the earliest origins of any form of racing, as chariot races were the first of the Olympic equestrian events. There is, however, very little similarity between the chariot – a weapon of war – and the *sulky*, a light two-wheeled vehicle with pneumatic tyres, which is used today. In addition the modern horses are not allowed to gallop but must either trot (when the legs move in diagonal pairs – right foreleg and left hindleg together) or pace (when the legs move in lateral pairs – left foreleg and left hindleg together).

Trotters are used for harness racing all over the world, but although the pacers are faster they are only popular in the USA, Australia, New Zealand and Italy. The fastest pacers go about 32m.p.h (51km.p.h.), which is almost as fast as top-class flat racers can gallop.

Harness racing started as an extra test for the horses of the eighteenth and nineteenth century that were used to pull light carriages for speedy travel before the advent of the motor car. Russia was one of the first countries to take the sport seriously and developed a special breed for it – the Orlov Trotter, named after their breeder, Count Orlov. America, too, produced her own breed, the foundation sire being the English Thoroughbred Messenger who was imported in 1788. The breed he founded became known as the Standardbred – known as such because all untried horses had to trot one mile in a standard time before being allowed to race. The early descendants of Messenger were raced on the track at a trot under saddle, not in harness, and it was not until the 1870s that the jockeys concentrated on gallopers and left trotters to pull *sulkies*.

In France trotting expanded fast after the opening of the first trotting track in Normandy in 1836. The French crossed their Norman mares with British Thoroughbreds and Norfolk Trotters to create a breed which became the mainstay of a sport which is now almost as popular as flat racing.

Harness racing is 'big business' today, with high prize money, luxurious tracks, huge numbers of regular spectators and large betting takes in such countries as Germany (more popular than flat racing),

Above: A Pacer on an Italian track. Note the lateral pairs of fore- and hindlegs moving together, whereas the Trotter moves his diagonal pairs together. (*Sylvester Jacobs*)

France, Italy, Australia, New Zealand, Russia and the USA. The latter, however, has long been considered supreme in harness racing – their horses are the fastest, Standardbreds holding the records, and the prizes are so vast that leading horses can win more than $1 500 000 (about £750 000) during their careers.

Quarter Horse racing

Quarter Horse racing was unique for a long time to the USA. It was the country's earliest form of racing, as was the breed, which was developed from Spanish and English stock to help the farmers and plantation owners in Virginia and the Carolinas during the eighteenth century. On weekends and holidays the best of these horses were tested in races, allegedly down the main street of the towns. These rough racetracks were necessarily short, usually about a quarter of a mile – hence the name of the breed.

Today the Quarter Horse is America's most numerous breed, and although the horses are used for a large number of purposes – on the ranch, in rodeos, for showing and trail riding – the best are still tested on the racetrack. With their exceptional powers of acceleration, derived largely from their powerful hindquarters, they are spectacular to watch and draw large crowds. The winners are handsomely rewarded: one of the richest races in the world is the All American Futurity for two-year-old Quarter Horses (worth about $400 000/£200 000) which is run at Ruidoso Downs, New Mexico each Labor Day.

Right, above: Rarus a famous American Trotting horse from the 1880s, a period when Harness Racing's popularity was growing fast. (*Peter Newark's Western Americana*)

Right, below: Harness racing is a sport which is at least as popular as flat racing in such countries as Italy, Germany, the US, and Australia. (*Sylvester Jacobs*)

Although Quarter Horse races have been run for more than 200 years, the first officially sanctioned race was not held until 1945. The American Quarter Horse Association became the controlling body and they now recognize 75 horse tracks which are straightaway courses just 400m (440yds) long. The A.Q.H.A. has also advised on the development of the sport elsewhere, for tracks are no longer confined to the USA, and the sport has spread to Canada and Mexico.

Races need not be over the full distance but can be as short as 200m. All races are started from a closed starting gate, and are over in seconds, for even the 400m takes good horses only about 22 seconds. This quick result seems to appeal to bettors for the annual betting take is close to $75 million (£38 million). This is the money which provides the sport with such high prizes – as in so many forms of racing it is the bettors who have turned it into a lucrative industry.

151

The Horse in the Arena

When rodeos started in the last century in America they were not performed in arenas, but were spontaneous contests put on by cowboys who had assembled and were looking for entertainment. These assemblies generally took place after roundups from the huge unfenced ranges of the West, or after cattle drives – when trail crews had to herd cattle from frontier country to railheads for shipment to the East. Huge numbers of cowboys would congregate and, in an effort to relieve the boredom of waiting for their cattle to be loaded on to the trains, or to celebrate the end of the roundup, they would stage informal contests based on cowboy skills – breaking horses, roping cattle etc., and bet their earnings on them.

These contests became increasingly formalized until on Independence Day (July 4), 1886, a rodeo was staged in front of paying spectators at Prescott in Arizona. It was the start of a major entertainment and eventually rodeos were staged in arenas which today hold spectators on three sides and on the fourth there is a row of chutes through which animals and contestants enter.

Formerly the major entertainment in cowboy country had been the Wild West show. These were more theatrical affairs containing circus-like displays of trick riding, shooting and roping; carnival-like exhibitions of Western folklore depicting events like the Indian massacres, and some contests like bull riding, steer wrestling and wagon races. The latter differed from rodeo activities in that they were not strictly ranch occupations.

Wild West shows were expensive to put on and lost many followers to the increasingly popular rodeos. Hence around 1900 rodeos and the Wild West shows merged, with the emphasis on competition rather than exhibition.

Today the rodeo is one of America's major forms of entertainment. Between 500 and 600 rodeos are sanctioned annually in the USA and Canada by the official ruling body, the Rodeo Cowboys Association. The events draw over 10 million spectators in a year and the contestants are well rewarded financially: the overall and all-round champions in the USA can earn about $100 000 (£50 000) each year.

Rodeo champions pay heavily for their high earnings. Apart from the huge expenses of entry fees, travelling and living costs, there is a physical toll. Their bodies take a terrible pounding and the pain-killing drug is all too often an unwelcome neccessity to get through each day. The rise towards the top, and the fall from, the rodeo ladder has become known as the Suicide Circuit. Professionals compete in up to 100 rodeos during the season which runs all year round. Less dedicated competitors concentrate on local rodeos like the Cheyenne Frontier Days or the Calgary Stampede.

The rodeo starts with the grand entry when contestants, judges and

officials ride into the arena dressed in colourful western attire. A band plays rousing music and it is a gay, picturesque start to rather rougher proceedings. There are five standard events – bareback riding, bull riding, saddle-bronc riding, calf roping and steer wrestling, but such events as barrel racing, team roping, steer roping and wild-cow milking are often included.

Calf roping is the only contest which has relevance to today's activities on the ranch. A calf is released into the arena through a chute. As soon as it crosses the score line the clock starts and the cowboy rides after it to try to lasso the animal. As soon as he succeeds the horse slides to a halt and backs up to keep the rope which is tied around the saddle horn tight. The cowboy leaps off and races to the calf to turn it on its side and tie three of its legs together. As soon as this is completed the clock is stopped, and the winning contestant is the man who achieves all this in the shortest time.

Steer wrestling (also referred to as *bulldogging*) is also judged on time. In this a steer is encouraged to gallop straight across the arena by a man on horseback known as a *hazer*. The contestant approaches the steer from the other side of the hazer and leaps from his horse to seize the steer's horns and head. He has to try to bring the steer to a halt by digging his boots into the ground, and then twisting its neck to

Above, left: An Australian trying his hand at buckjumping at the end of last century. This contest was a feature of rodeos and wild west shows. (*Peter Newark's Historical Pictures*)

Above, right: This cowboy is calf roping on a ranch but this work has been adapted into a contest staged at rodeos. (*Janet Kidd*)

153

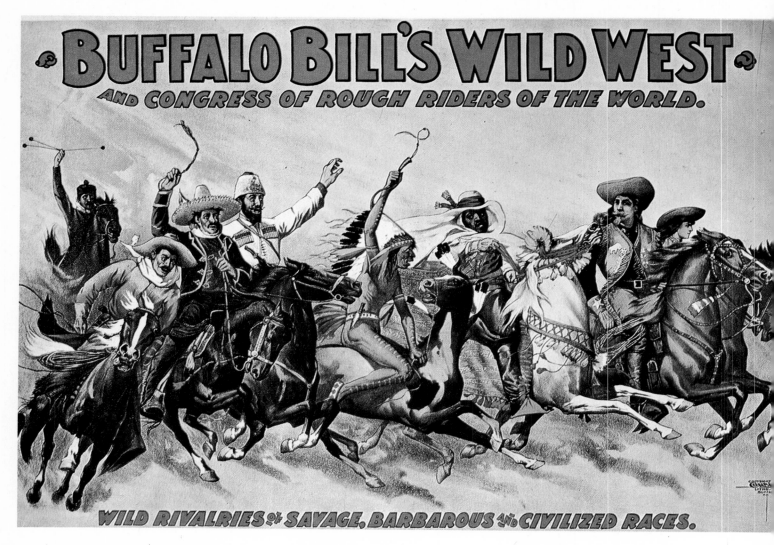

force it to the ground. The clock is stopped as soon as the steer has been wrestled to the ground.

The riding contests are decided on a points system. Mounted judges in the arena score the contestant's ride taking into account both the ferocity of the animal's bucks and whirls and the skills of the rider. The rider has to remain on the animal for a specified time. This is usually 8 to 10 seconds, and if he survives a pickup man rides alongside the animal to help the contestant off. If he is thrown before the time-limit expires or if in the bareback or saddle-bronc events the competitor touches either the saddle, surcingle or the horse with the hand he is supposed to keep free, then he is eliminated.

The animal used can be a horse – known as a bronc – or a bull. The bronc may be ridden bareback, when there is just a surcingle strap with a leather handhold, or in a modified stock saddle when the rider must keep his feet in the stirrups. In *bull riding* the contestant is allowed to use both hands to clutch the surcingle's handhold.

In *bareback bronc riding* the contestant must spur his mount on the shoulders in the first leap out of the chute, and he will earn high marks from the judges if he continues to spur his bronc during the performance.

Team roping is one of the more common of the minor rodeo events. In this two men work together, one roping the steer's head and the other the steer's hind legs. Then there are some more humorous events like *wild-cow milking*, when a team of two cowboys try to catch a highly

Above: A poster for one of the Wild West shows at the end of the nineteenth century. The Wild West show was the forerunner of the rodeo. (*Peter Newark's Western Americana*)

Above, right: Bronc riders can try their hand bareback. Note the contestant spurring his horse to try and earn higher points, and the bucking strap around the horse's flank. (*Peter Newark's Western Americana*)

Right, below: A rodeo at South Dakota where one bareback bronc rider takes a spectacular fall. (*Peter Newark's Western Americana*)

154

Above: London Horse shows at the end of last century and the beginning of the twentieth were very fashionable affairs. This style of showing horses 'in hand', using long reins instead of leading them, is no longer practised. (*Mary Evans Picture Library*)

unco-operative cow. One then hangs on to the cow while the other, faced with kicking hind legs and a lashing tail, has to perform the dangerous task of extracting a few drops of milk. When a dribble of milk has been collected in a bottle the contestants leave the cow and race for the finishing line.

The *wild horse race* is as amusing for spectators as it is muddling and dangerous for contestants. Eight to ten broncs are released from the chutes and the contestants, each helped by two assistants, have to capture a horse, saddle and then ride him to the other end of the arena.

The ladies join in the rather less dangerous activity of *barrel racing*. Contestants race individually around barrels set in a triangular pattern. The winner is the person with the fastest time.

These contests are usually interspaced with exhibitions of trick riding and roping, and at some rodeos there are chuck-wagon and chariot races. The youngsters can join the action too, for they can be asked to capture a goat or a greased pig.

In America most of the rodeos are held under the auspices of the Rodeo Cowboys Association, although there are quite a number of more amateurish affairs arranged by colleges, schools and for dude ranch vacationers.

In Australia the sport is controlled by the Australian Rough Riders Association which has more than 12000 members. Their rodeos are held almost all year round – in the southern states in the summer months, and further north in the winter. The contests are much the same as those in the USA although a variation on cutting an animal from the herd called camdrafting is popular. In this the animal is released from the yard and then has to be kept on a cloverleaf-shaped course by the contestant.

Above: In eastern Europe and Asia there are a variety of games played on horseback in arenas. This one is being staged in Moscow. (*Robert Harding Associates*)

The show ring

The show world is on the opposite end of the equestrian spectrum to the rodeo, for show horses are pampered creatures and beauty is all important. The most handsome animals are selected as winners by the judge or judges in show classes, although other factors such as training, the ride they give and style of jumping can also be taken into account.

There are a host of different classes from foals and ponies to massive, heavyweight hunters, and from light, elegant Arabs to fancily-turned-out Parade horses. The types of horse shown and the features looked for by the judges vary greatly from country to country. Showing is very much a national affair reflecting the type of horses bred and the uses they are put to.

Although a judge will look for particular features in different classes show horses do have certain common features. It is vital that the show horse has excellent conformation (shape), be well-proportioned and

Above: Competitors at Britain's Royal International Horse Show wait in the collecting ring before they enter the arena for final judging. (*Sylvester Jacobs*)

have no weak parts to the body. An elegant head is a great asset, as is a graceful crested neck, a sloping shoulder, a deep broad chest, a back that is neither too long or too short, muscular, powerful hindquarters and strong limbs which are placed squarely under the body.

Straight, active movement is essential, as is good temperament which enables the horse to remain calm during the hurly-burly of the shows and the tests which he is put through. On the other hand he must be alert, and show what is known as 'presence'. A horse with presence demands attention: he is cocky, takes a great interest in activities around him and appears to enjoy, rather than merely submit to, his rider's demands.

The final common denominator for showing around the world is that the horse is well-turned-out. He must be well-fed, so that he looks healthy, he must have been consistently groomed so that the coat gleams, have a neatly plaited/braided mane, oiled hooves, polished tack and a rider who has taken as great pains over his own appearance and clothes, as he did with his horse. Showing does entail 'showing off', and every aspect of the contestants must be made as beautiful as possible.

In Britain where hunting plays such a major part in equestrian activities it is the hunter classes which feature at the shows held from late April until the grand finale at the Horse of the Year Show in early

Above: Classes for Costers Turnouts are colourful and popular. The wagons are always laden with fruit and flowers. (*Sylvester Jacobs*)

October. Since all sizes and shapes of horses are used to follow hounds there are quite a number of hunter divisions – the small hunter (under 15.2hh); the lightweight (for a light rider); the middleweight; the heavyweight; and the ladies' hunter (ridden side-saddle). These hunters are all judged for their conformation (they must be the type to remain sound when faced with the rigours of hunting); movement (the gallop is especially important); ride (they must be comfortable as they should be able to carry a rider for hours across country); and good manners. Another division has been added – the working hunter, in which contestants have to prove they can perform as well as look beautiful by jumping fences.

Hunters are used for sport, and need to be bold and strong, but in the past elegant horses were needed for more sedate activities and these were known as hacks. They were used for gentle hacks in the country and in particular to show off with in Hyde Park's Rotten Row. Fashion-conscious aristocrats in the last century and early this century needed to prove how dignified they looked on horseback and how well-trained their horses were. This tradition is continued today by the hack classes in the show ring. The hack must be pretty, not as powerful as a hunter, he must have an eye-catching trot but does not need to gallop, and his canter must be very slow and so comfortable that riders can still carry on a conversation.

159

Above: Mounted Games are some of the most popular arena competitions for children. They include such games as bending races and apple bobbing. (*Sylvester Jacobs*)

Like the hunter, there are various divisions of hacks: small; large, which is still under 15.3hh; and ladies, which is ridden side-saddle.

The third major section of Britain's show world is the pony. The tough Mountain and Moorland breeds of pony have been crossed with small Thoroughbreds and Arabs to produce pretty ponies for children to ride. Although the major requisites are again conformation and movement, manners play a very important part as the ponies should be suitable for youngsters to ride.

The smallest division is for ponies of 12.2hh and under, to be ridden by children who are twelve years old or less. The largest is for ponies of 13.2hh to 14.2hh, to be ridden by children between fourteen and sixteen. These ponies are merely shown off on the flat, but like the hunters there are divisions for working ponies, who have to show that they are capable of jumping as well as looking pretty.

There are show classes for those charming burly horses – Cobs, and for all the various pure-bred horses found in Britain (Arabs, Cleveland Bays etc.). These classes for breeds are further divided into sections for brood mares and foals, lead yearlings, two-year-olds and stallions, and for ridden older horses.

In America, however, there is an even greater range of show classes with more than forty different types of division. They have some of the most spectacular and flamboyant show classes in the world. The Parade divisions are the most colourful and least professional, for riding ability is hardly taken into account. In these, contestants are judged largely on turnout so riders wear lavish costumes and the saddlery is bedecked with silver and jewelled embellishments. The amateur rider can also do well in the Costume classes which are fancy dress on horseback, and in the Pleasure classes when the horses are judged on their ease of handling, manners and suitability to the rider.

Most of the other show classes are dominated by the professional rider or at least the professionally-trained rider. The show classes have become such an important feature of American shows that big money is involved, both in prizes and in the escalating value of prizewinners.

The most popular classes with the general public are the divisions for horses with unusual and spectacular gaits like the Tennessee Walkers and the Saddlebreds. The Tennessee Walker's running walk is a crowd-puller, for the hind legs over-reach the forelegs to an unusual extent, the legs come high in the air and the horse travels at great speed. The five-gaited Saddlebreds perform a slow gait which is a prancing motion in four-time. Each hoof is lifted and remains suspended before being returned to the ground. The *rack* is a speeded up version of this which makes it even more spectacular to watch.

The Western Division classes are some of the most practical in the USA. They are staged at shows specializing entirely in these events or form part of the varied programme of the American Horse Shows Association shows.

The Western classes are supposed to simulate ranch activities, and consequently the same type of horses (Quarter Horses, Appaloosas, Paints, Morgans and Arabs), the same gear (cowboy clothes, a stock saddle with a horn, high cantle, wide, thick leather fenders and stirrup leathers, and a bridle with a Western-style curb bit with long shanks or a hackamore or bosal), and the same style of riding (long stirrups and loose reins held in one hand) are used.

The Stock Horse section tests the skill of contestants in ranch work. They may be asked to perform a Western-style dressage test, known as a reining test, which contains such movements as a figure of eight with flying changes and a sliding stop from a full gallop. Then they can be asked to work cattle and to manoeuvre a calf or steer according to the judges' instructions.

The Trail Horse section tests the ability of the horse to carry his rider safely across country. He must perform a test on a relatively loose rein, get through such obstacles as an expanse of water, a pile of logs, or a bridge and be able to open and close a gate.

In the Pleasure section the contestants show off their gaits and manners. Then after working both ways in the arena the judges assess the conformation and the standard of behaviour (manners) of the horses.

The Western Division classes are most popular in the home territory of the cowboy in the West and Florida, but in the East the Hunter plays a more important role than the cow pony, and show classes for it are consequently plentiful at the East Coast shows. The various classes in the Hunter Division test conformation, manners and the athletic talents needed to follow hounds across country. Much more emphasis is put on jumping ability in America than Britain, and it has to be proven in style. It is not sufficient to merely clear a fence; it has to be done calmly, with rhythm and a fluent jump in which the horse rounds its back and lowers its head. This entails a lot of training before production in the show ring, but it is time well-spent for, helped by this groundwork, many of the American show hunters go on to make excellent show jumpers or event horses.

Above: The Tennessee Walking Horse is able to perform spectacular gaits which are fast yet comfortable for the rider. Arena classes to judge action, conformation and manners are popular in the US. (*Sally Anne Thompson*)

There are numerous classes within the Hunter division but all horses usually start as Green hunters and the best progress to the Open (which can be divided into lightweight, middleweight and heavyweight), whereas the others can try local, ladies, junior, amateur owners etc. classes. There are also Hunter classes for ponies, so practically every type of Hunter has a class to suit him.

There are a large number of driving classes which include some for Hackneys, with their high spectacular trot, and for Roadsters, where speed plays a more important part in the judging. Then there are some classes for purebreds and those which get the most entries are the 'all American' Quarter Horse and the elegant historical Arab.

No other country has such a range of showing classes as America, but the Australians do put on a good number of classes especially at their magnificent Royal Shows of Sydney and Melbourne which are run in palatial establishments. Hack, Best Rider Turnout, In Hand Breed classes, Harness horses and ponies, Parade, Costume and Stockhorse classes are run in a multitude of rings.

South Africans organize specialized shows for Hackneys, Saddlebreds and Arabs in addition to running classes for them, hacks, riding horses and working ponies at most of their major shows.

Left: American Saddlebreds are shown in all types of classes. On this occasion they are showing off their speed when being driven. (*Sally Anne Thompson*)

Below: Hackneys with their spectacular action at the trot are a popular form of show class. These are just being brought forward for the prize giving. (*Sylvester Jacobs*)

163

The bull ring

Showing horses is one of the most sedate and safe equestrian activities; bullfighting must be one of the most dangerous. Bulls were originally fought from horseback but today there are all too few horsemen (known as *rejoneadores*) who fight bulls. Apart from the skill of fighting the bull in the arena, it takes years of training talented horses to turn them into relatively reliable assistants for this dangerous art.

The horse has to be trained to be a combination between a cow pony, which can whirl around, stop instantly and accelerate rapidly into a fast gallop; and a High School horse, which can perform exotic movements like the Spanish walk, *passage* and *capriole* – a leap into the air. This takes time and it is only after the movements have been mastered that a horse can be tested with the bulls to discover whether he has those other essential assets – courage and obedience when faced with a charging bull.

The *rejoneador*'s typical performance starts with a flamboyant display of High School. Usually riding an Andalusian stallion, he will perform the most spectacular movements like *passage* and *piaffe* and will sometimes even canter backwards, and bow as he is applauded.

After this colourful display of horsemanship the serious business begins and the *rejoneador* changes to a faster horse ready for the entry of the bull. He needs to tire his adversary so in an exciting few minutes he gallops around and around the arena, drawing the bull on and keeping just ahead of him. When the bull is ready to stand still in the middle of the arena he leaves him there and with the *rejon* (which ends in a blade) in his hand, he turns to face the *toro*. They charge at each other and the horse veers away far enough to avoid the horns but close enough for the *rejoneador* to drive the *rejon* into the bull's withers.

Three *rejons* are inserted in this manner and then the horse is changed (again). Since the bull is tiring less speed is needed but manoeuvrability is essential, for the shorter *banderillas* now have to be inserted. To do this the horse might approach the bull in the Spanish walk, then break into a charge and swing only fractionally away from the bull. Sometimes the *rejoneador* has such a good horse that he can let his reins loose during this manoeuvre and concentrate on placing his pair of *banderillas* into the bull.

Then it is another change of horse for the final stages and the kill. The long, thin *rejon de muerte* is the weapon used for this dramatic operation and the horse has to be exceptionally obedient to allow the *rejoneador* to achieve a clean kill. One of the closest relationships between man and horse is needed for successful bullfighting on horseback.

The circus ring

Circus riders are showmen who entertain the public by training their horses to perform complicated, pretty and unusual manoeuvres. Dancing horses were described in Roman times as were equestrian displays at fairs in later years, but the original circus equestrian exhibition in its own arena was the work of Philip Astley in the eighteenth century. In a London amphitheatre, which was a combination of the palatial riding schools built in Europe at that time and the music halls which were fashionable in Britain, Astley ran very popular, rather dignified, equestrian displays.

With the decline of exotic court life in Europe and the consequent loss of venues for the popular High School shows of the seventeenth and eighteenth century, the circus movement spread across the Channel. Two of the greatest horsemen of the nineteenth century – Baucher and Fillis – were circus riders in France. Their performances in the various permanent circus amphitheatres around Europe and Russia, where Fillis moved to at the end of his career, were the scenes of many great displays of horsemanship.

Today circuses have been criticized by the equestrian 'establishment' as highly artificial: the horse is used as an entertainer who bows and dances instead of retaining his dignity by being asked to perform only movements based on his natural abilities, as in dressage. The rejoinder to this is that the 1976 Olympic gold medallist and 1978 World Champion in dressage, Christine Stuckelberger was helped greatly in training by one of the world's greatest circus performers – Freddie Knie. The two activities are not as far apart as many critics suggest.

The most popular breeds in the circus are the intelligent, powerful Lipizzaners, the elegant, lightfooted Arabs and the round, springy

Above, left: A High School display at the circus. The nearest horse is performing the Spanish Walk, a movement which is considered too artificial to be included in dressage tests. (*Sylvester Jacobs*)

Above, right: One of the most famous arenas in the world is the Spanish Riding School in Vienna. In it an elite group of horsemen demonstrate to the world how to ride High School. (*Herz Color Verlag*)

Right: A horseback display at a fair. These are much rarer than in the past, for most of the riders who have such skills join circuses. (*Sylvester Jacobs*)

Andalusians. They are breeds which are rarely successful in dressage tests for although they may be spectacular to watch, their paces lack the scope needed for vital extensions.

There are three basic types of circus horse; those used for vaulting, for High School and for Liberty acts. Vaulting horses are also called resinbacks because of the resin put on their backs to stop the vaulters from slipping. They are usually rather big horses with flat backs, a smooth rhythmical canter and quiet temperaments. Their most essential quality is that they can keep cantering at the same speed despite the frantic acts of clowns, who might even hang onto their tails, and the gymnastic performances of the jockeys who carry out all manner of complicated manoeuvres as they leap on and off their horses' backs during the act.

166

Liberty horses are usually matched, small and pretty. They are taught, at first on the lunge, to become totally obedient to cues and to the voice of their trainer. They perform without riders but are clad in eye-catching harness and often have plumes on their backs and between their ears. Although Liberty acts usually consist of a group of six or more horses, sometimes one of them proves to be particularly talented and will perform more exotic movements like *piaffe* or a *capriole* on its own.

The High School horse is ridden by a decoratively-clad trainer and usually performed solo. Each performance is the individual creation of the trainer and apart from the traditional dressage movements like *piaffe* and *passage*, the horse might dance to music; some can even manage to step in time to a waltz or a tango.

The greatest equestrian acts of present time are those of the Knie circus which is based in Switzerland. It boasts of an enormous collection of horses ranging from Shetland ponies to the golden Akhal Teke stallions from Russia. Britain's Mary Chipperfield and her family's circus is gaining increasing renown for her Liberty and High School acts. In Germany the Circus Krone and Barum-Safari run outstanding equestrian acts. In America there is the biggest circus in the world – the Ringling-Barnum – which runs three rings so that three acts, usually identical, can be performed simultaneously. This is a spectacular operation but demanding on the concentration and obedience of those wonderfully-trained horses.

The horse is a remarkable creature – he serves man in so many ways. He provides aesthetic pleasure, he carries man in all manner of sports, and in the circus he is turned into an entertainer who can perform breathtaking tricks.

The Horse at Work

Although the horse has been an essential assistant to man at work, over the last century he has been made redundant from most of his tasks. Once a vital part of the productive process before mechanization, he is now used mainly to help man fill his leisure hours and further his sporting ambitions. As such he has become more subject to affection, and his welfare is of great importance. This is a very different role from the past when he was usually little more than a tool being used as an instrument of war, a source of power or a means of transport.

The horse in the army

The horse began his work for man as an instrument of war. From the time the Aryans first discovered how to harness the horse to chariots and the contribution this made in their conquests of their neighbours, until the disastrous cavalry charges of the Poles and the Cossacks in World War II, the horse has been vital in army work. Although World War II proved, to great cost in human and equine lives, that the horse no longer had a role in the forefront of battle, he is still used in the armies of the world.

Some countries still maintain a working cavalry for, in mountainous areas, such as those of Switzerland, transportation of guns etc. by horse is more efficient than using mechanized means. Even in countries where the terrain does not make horses necessary, small mounted units are maintained. In unique circumstances they might be used for fighting but their major role is ceremonial.

In Britain the squadrons of the Life Guards, the Blues and Royals and the King's Troop of the Royal Horse Artillery add pageantry to every occasion in which they participate, and are a reminder of the army's past when they were dependent on the horse.

All over the world countries maintain small units of mounted troops. Again, they are used for ceremonial purposes, and, when they are dressed in their glamorous uniforms of the past, they add a particularly distinguished and colourful note. Fortunately the horrifying predicaments that all too often faced the horse in war – disease, starvation and injury during charges – are now part of the past.

The horse in agriculture

When we think of a work horse, it is usually of the huge, magnificent animals that pulled the ploughs and are now such popular exhibition horses at the shows and competitors in ploughing matches. The surprising thing is that although these massive Coldbloods were for a time the farmers' major assistants, they were used for a relatively short period in history.

Oxen were the farmers' early workers on the land. These cumbersome, powerful animals could be driven in a yoke which was a wooden bar linking the two animals side by side and attached to them with straps. This system was painful to a horse as the straps passed in front of the neck and restricted his breathing. Because of this, early farmers could not harness the horse's pulling power.

The Chinese got around this problem by inventing a collar which was a pad going around the horse's neck and to which loads could be attached. The full force of the load could then fall on the horse's chest and shoulders which are muscular areas and his wind would not be restricted. The collar thus enabled the horse to pull great loads, and gave man a much more manoeuvrable means of transporting heavy materials than the ox.

It took some time to realize all the implications of this invention, for although the Chinese first used the collar before AD500, it was more than 300 years before it was adopted in Europe. Even then it was used mainly for horses and ponies to pull wagons, and it was not until well into the Middle Ages that farmers began to be converted to using the horse for ploughing. The effectiveness of the collar was not the only incentive for this change; also instrumental was the fact that the horse's strength was increasing. Heavier, more powerful horses were being developed to carry heavily-laden knights into battle, and some of these became available for tilling the land.

Above: In Ireland horses are still kept by most of the farmers and used for such work as collecting seaweed from the beaches. (*E Preston*)

169

Above: Last century the farmers relied almost entirely on horses to pull their ploughs. Today the magnificent heavy horses rarely work the land except in competitions like this ploughing match. (*Sylvester Jacobs*)

Many farmers were reluctant to carry out this form of modernization, however, for oxen were cheaper to feed than the working horse; it was not until the seventeenth century that the majority of British farmers were converted to the horse and the ox still prevailed in hotter climates.

It has been suggested that the Scandinavians used the horse to pull ploughs long before any other European people. This may have been because at the height of the Viking Age the Norsemen wanted to spend as much of the summer as possible plundering the coastlines of Europe. They had to get their farms tilled rapidly if they were going to have the time to carry out their adventurous plans, so to speed up the process they replaced the pedantic ox with the faster, more manoeuvrable horse.

Light work on the farms had been done by horses and ponies for centuries. Harrowing had long been a horse's work, for it needed only very rudimentary harness to pull this light load. There is evidence that in some cases a crude harrow was fashioned by attaching thorn bushes to the horse's tail.

Horses also performed extremely mundane tasks before the advent of the steam engine. They plodded around and around, turning wheels to which they were harnessed in order to raise water or operate threshing machines.

The eighteenth century was a creative period when farmers benefited from improved harrows, hoes, rollers, drills, ploughs and the invention

of reaping and mowing machines. For all of these the power of the horse was essential. To increase this power horses were bred larger and larger and teams of horses were sometimes used. In America, Canada and Australia, where in the huge open prairies there were no gates to restrict width, up to a dozen horses might be harnessed side by side to make up teams of thirty or more to pull heavy harvesting machines and gang ploughs.

The other area of agriculture in which the horse was essential was forestry. The inaccessibility of some forests, such as those in Finland, means that the horse is still of value in this sphere.

Even today the horse has not been completely abandoned as an agricultural aid. In some industrialized nations fuel shortages have encouraged a few farmers to return to this old source of power. Amongst the nations where small farmers need power for a wide range of jobs – ploughing, pulling, reaping etc. – the various machines necessary might be too expensive; hence the versatile horse, or at least the tough pony or mule is still in action. The horse is still an essential part of agricultural production in underdeveloped countries such as Indonesia and in mountainous farms like those of Eastern Europe.

The horse has been used for herding animals for a longer time than for any other purpose. Mounted herdsmen of modern times include the Cumberland shepherd on his Fell pony, the Australian stockman, the cowboys in France's Camargue region who round up those fierce black

Above: One of the major rôles of the few remaining mounted soldiers is to add colour, dignity and tradition to parades. The Horse Guards on their black horses perform this function well. (*Sylvester Jacobs*)

171

The Horse at Work

Right: A Norwegian Fjord pony in harness, taking a break between moving loads of hay. (*E Preston*)

172

bulls, the Argentinians who care for huge herds of beef cattle on their tough Criollos, the American cowboys in the West on their powerful, versatile Quarter Horses, and the Czikos (cowboys) in Hungary who look after the herds on their plains on horseback. In the wide open spaces of the prairies and plains nothing as fast, manoeuvrable or tough as the horse has been found for inspecting, driving, rounding up, and cutting individual animals from a herd.

The horse in industry

The horse might have had to work hard in agriculture, but at least he retained his dignity, working in the open air and being looked after by people who understood animals. Sadly, all too often in industry man turned him into a machine performing repetitive, heavy duties in a bad environment. The horse played an essential rôle in the industrialization of our nations, but we cannot be proud of what we made the horse do in our quest for progress.

The horse was a source of power before the advent of the motor engine. Horse-power, not steam, was used to operate early machines. He was made to turn the windlass of the hoist at the pitheads of coal mines, he pulled wagons along early railways, he was a substitute for windmills to raise water from the ground, and by making him plod around and around for hours on end he could be used as a means of pumping, drilling, turning etc., all of which were vital for the manufacturing industries.

The invention of steam power relieved him of many of these onerous duties but the need for coal to produce this steam led to increased demands on the horse to be used in mining. Man had to dig deeper to produce more, and many miles of tunnels were constructed in the coal mines. Railway tracks were built through them so that coal could be hauled in wagons from the coalface to the pithead. From the nineteenth century up to recent times horses, or at least little ponies, were found to be the most efficient hauliers of these wagons. There were more than 20 000 pit ponies in full work in 1946, and although today modern machinery has made most redundant, there are still a small number carrying on this dirty, unhealthy but essential work.

Small size was vital for work in the pits so it was the powerful minute Shetlands and the tough Icelandic ponies that were most commonly used. Many of them lived in underground stables, and were only brought to the surface for an occasional holiday.

The horse as transport

It is in the sphere of transportation that the horse has made his greatest practical contribution. At first he did this by carrying individuals, providing them with a speedy means of transport which could take them further afield, and by acting as a pack animal to carry their heavier goods and belongings. This work is still performed by the horse, especially in the mountainous and underdeveloped areas where roads are either impossible or too expensive to build.

Much of the pack-work, especially in hot climates, is done by the horse's near relation – the mule. The mule, which is the offspring of a mare by a jackass, has long been used for this work. It is claimed that

Below: Mustering cattle in Australia. Cowboys were just as important in the huge open lands of Australia as they were in the US. (*Peter Newark's Historical Pictures*)

Opposite: A working cowboy from the 1880s. There have been few changes over the ensuing hundred years to the equipment, clothes or horses used. (*Peter Newark's Western Americana*)

Above: On the ranches out West in the US horses were, and still are, assistants to the cowboys. They were roughly and quickly trained for their work by such methods as those depicted in Frederic Remington's drawing. (*Peter Newark's Western Americana*)

the ass, a native of hot climates, was tamed and used by man for transportation before the horse.

The more efficient use of the horse for transportation by getting him to pull far greater loads than he could carry, was made possible with the inventions of the wheel and the collar, and by the construction of better roads in Roman times. The Romans did begin to use heavy four-wheeled wagons drawn by horses for transportation but rather surprisingly the idea was not generally adopted until well into the Middle Ages.

It has been suggested that the era of the horse-drawn vehicle – wagons (for goods) and coaches (for mail and passengers) – began in Hungary in the town of Kotsee, from which the name coach is derived. In England the first coach was built for the Earl of Rutland, in the middle of the sixteenth century, and a few years later, in 1564, one was brought to England from Holland for Queen Elizabeth. It must have been a success because a state coach was then built and used in 1571 for the Opening of Parliament, and soon most of those who could afford it were making use of this convenient means of transport.

The spread of the use of the coach did not meet with universal approval. There were some who thought this swing towards driving rather than riding was effeminate, and likely to lead to such a deterioration in horsemanship that a bill to restrict coaching was introduced in Parliament in 1601. It was, however, unsuccessful and the swing continued.

The coach did not remain the province of the rich for too long for by the mid seventeenth century stage-coaches were in operation. These ran along specified routes at scheduled times to collect and carry the general public and their luggage. A long journey was completed in a series of stages, the horses being changed and the passengers sleeping at coaching inns.

Above: In Australia large numbers of horses escaped to the Bush to roam and breed wild. This shows a herd being 'run in'. (*Peter Newark's Historical Pictures*)

These journeys for the early passengers were pretty hazardous. The roads were very rough and so muddy in winter that coaching was confined to summertime. Then there were the highwaymen, who regularly earned their income by holding up the coaches.

Improvements were gradually made. Coaches were sprung to make them more comfortable and more extensive use of the roads led to better protection against highwaymen. But, probably most important of all, in 1818 John Macadam's idea of laying relatively small (less than 6oz/170g) uniform stones to a depth of 6in (152mm) to act as a road foundation was put into effect. The result was that the coaches travelled more easily and lighter, faster horses could be used. Macadamized roads heralded what became known as the Golden Age of Coaching when increased comforts and greater speeds (the average speed was about 10m.p.h.) led to enormous numbers of coaches hurrying all over the British Isles.

Many of the improvements were due to the great competition for passengers between the Stage and Mail coaches. The Mail coach had its first run on 2nd August 1784, and made a journey from Bristol and Bath to London. This momentous trip was made on the instigation of a theatre manager, John Palmer, who brought much pressure to bear on the government. Palmer claimed that the mounted post-boys who delivered the post were slower and much more vulnerable to attack

from highwaymen than a coach carrying armed guards. At Palmer's expense this first mail coach was run, and it did deliver the post faster than the post-boys so the idea was adopted on other routes.

In 1804 the first passengers were carried to help supplement the income of mail coaches. One passenger was carried on the box seat alongside the coachman, three more sat on a forward-facing seat behind the coachman and four people could ride inside. The guard rode on a seat at the back, and had at hand a blunderbuss, pistols and the coach horn. Blasts on this long horn were used to warn other road users to get out of the way, for turnpike-keepers to have the gates open, and for the ostlers at the inns to have the horses in position for a rapid change.

Speed was a vital factor both in the delivery of mail and to encourage customers to choose the mail, rather than the stage-coach, for travel. The Mails (as they were known), had advantages in this and other spheres for they had the right of way over all other road users. They were untaxed and paid no tolls. By 1835 there were about 700 of these privileged users of the roads.

By the late 1830s the Golden Age of Coaching was over for the railways were providing a speedier means of travel. The steam engine had been developed and replaced the horses which had pulled wagons along the early railways.

In America the stage-coach did not face much competition from the

steam-powered railways until much later. For much of the nineteenth century communications depended largely on the special American stage-coach – a four-wheeled vehicle which was slung on leather thoroughbraces (strong straps on which the vehicle rested and which were fastened to standards at each end). Four or six horses used to pull these coaches across the wild open country during the opening up of America.

The railway might have made the stage and mail horse redundant in Britain but private coaches were in constant use in the nineteenth century; and in the city the horse still played 'the' most important role in transportation. At the end of the nineteenth century there were more than 300000 horses in London alone.

More than 12000 of these horses were the property of the London General Omnibus Company. The Omnibus was a relatively new form of

Above: The Manchester Day Coach drawn by a team of greys in 1834, towards the end of Britain's golden age of coaching. (*Peter Newark's Historical Pictures*)

transport originating in Paris in 1819 when Jacques Laffitte designed a horse-drawn bus, and named it an omnibus, meaning a bus for all people. With up to twenty-two seats, they were a more efficient means of public transport than the existing coaches and carts. They were introduced to London in 1829 by George Shillibeer and he provided a luxurious service with coachmen dressed in velvet suits and a library on board to help relieve the boredom of travel. Rival firms, however, were more economical and their cheaper fares meant that eventually Shillibeer was forced out of business.

The different companies painted the omnibuses in their own colours, and vied with each other to attract customers by establishing the best reputation for speed and comfort. The resulting excessive competition produced take-over bids and by 1904 The London General Omnibus Company controlled three-quarters of London's buses.

179

For the omnibus horse it was a hard, dreary existence. He had to be strong and surefooted for as one of a pair he had to pull up to three and a half tonnes of omnibus over roughly-paved streets, and continually stop and start at the commands of the passengers. Few omnibus horses could take this work for more than five years and many died in service.

The original trams were horse-drawn and this was an even harder task, as the trams were heavier and carried more passengers than the omnibus.

Nor did the cab (abbreviation from *cabriolet*, a manoeuvrable French carriage) horse have an easy existence. They were driven in pairs or singles mainly to the two-wheeled Hansom Cabs and the four-wheeled Clarence Cabs. At the end of the nineteenth century there were about 15000 horses performing these duties around London. They did not last for long, usually not more than three years for they hauled their cabs six days a week and up to 40 miles (64km) a day. When they were not pulling customers they had to wander along the streets searching for them or stand at one of the 600 cab stands waiting to pick up a fare.

When the load was goods rather than humans, speed was not such an essential factor so the stronger, slower, massive Coldbloods – the Shires and the Clydesdales – could be used. They collected refuse, hauled coal, loads of which could weigh three tons (3045kg), and transported brewers' barrels. At the end of the last century there were about 3000 heavy horses in London, owned by the large breweries. The

brewer's van weighed about seven tons (7105kg) laden, so the horses usually worked together in pairs or threes to haul this huge weight.

Today magnificent teams of black Shires or elegant grey Percherons are still seen in London hauling brewery drays. This practice was maintained mainly for publicity reasons as they catch attention on the streets, and can be exhibited at leading shows; however, the fuel crisis is once again turning the horse into an economical means of delivering beer.

The horse's other major use in transportation was in the pre-railway era when a network of canals was constructed for the transportation of raw materials and finished goods. The barges that carried these goods were towed by horses wherever there was a path alongside the canal. One horse plodding along the towpath was able to pull two boats about 21m (70ft) long and about 2m (7ft) wide.

The police horse

The horse's most responsible rôle is in maintaining law and order. The dangers of this rôle have been considerably reduced since the sheriffs of America's Wild West used the horse to chase after bandits. Some are still used for tracking and capturing criminals in Africa and South America, but the police horse's major rôles are now performed in the cities.

Above: This stagecoach is on a trip out West in the US, but the well-dressed ladies and gentlemen look ill equipped for the rigours of such a journey. (*Peter Newark's Western Americana*)

Overleaf: Britain's canals were once a major transport route for the country's industrial goods. The horses walked alongside pulling heavy barges like this one on the Kennet and Avon canal. (*Ivan Belcher*)

Above: The car has not replaced the horse completely as shown by this horse-drawn cart travelling along a Turkish street. (*E. Preston*)

The greatest blow to the reputation of the police horse was when their most famous users, the Royal Canadian Mounted Police, decided that the most efficient way of achieving their boast 'always get their man' was by using helicopters in inaccessible areas rather than the horse. When the Mounties were founded in 1873 as a semi-military force they were known as the North West Mounted Police. They had an enormous beat and their major task was to control more than 30000 Indians who could be very dangerous in the face of increasing encroachment from the White man. In addition they worked in wild country which made it an even more difficult task but they succeeded and the red coat became a symbol of security.

In 1920 the North West Mounted Police took over the policing of the whole of Canada and were given their present title of the Royal Canadian Mounted Police, but with this change came increasing mechanization. Today they use their black and dark brown horses only for ceremonial occasions and for their colourful and spectacular musical ride which they stage around the world.

Not all the police forces are in agreement with this discarding of the horse as a valuable instrument in the maintenance of law and order. For all its modernity New York maintains the largest mounted police force in the world. In London, where the first mounted police were members of the Bow Street Patrol of 1805, more than 200 horses are kept in the Metropolitan area. These London police horses still perform their original role of patrolling the streets and parks to keep them safe for law-abiding citizens. They also take part in most of the major ceremonies supplementing the horses of the Household Cavalry and the King's Troop. Two mounted policemen always escort new ambassadors when they present their credentials to the Queen at Buckingham Palace, and they are always on duty outside the Palace during the changing of the guard. However, perhaps a police horse's proudest duty is to carry the Queen during the Trooping of the Colour. A horse with an excellent temperament and dignified bearing is selected and trained to carry a side saddle, and some, like Winston and Imperial, become public personalities in their own right when they have performed this ceremony on a number of occasions.

In Australia the early mounted police were known as Trooper police and led a pretty dangerous existence. They were formed in Brisbane in 1826, but their most worthwhile early activities were in the country. They helped to protect the early settlers and travellers from bush-whackers and cattle thieves. Today, of course, the country is much safer and so the mounted forces have been reduced and concentrated in the cities.

All around the world most major cities maintain small forces. Apart from their ceremonial and patrolling duties they are important in the control of traffic. In traffic jams the extra height means that the police can see and be seen, and can wend their way between cars and onto the pavement or sidewalk to the source of the problem. In many countries they are also used to control street crossings.

By far the most effective work of the mounted policemen today is in the control of crowds. Horses are very successful dispersers of crowds and people on their feet are usually frightened into behaving when faced with a horse or horses charging towards them. Political demonstrations might be the most dangerous situations in terms of mob-power, but some sporting fixtures draw so many spectators that their crowds can get out of control. Thus mounted policemen are used at football matches and the more popular race meetings around the world.

The police horse must have an excellent temperament and be well-trained in order to do his work of facing angry mobs, or remaining calm in traffic and during colourful, gay occasions, and to be able to react quickly to the policeman's commands. This training includes elementary dressage work plus nuisance training when the horses are accustomed to the noise, emotional stress and disturbances they will have to meet.

This training turns the police horse into one which can give displays. Most of the mounted forces further public relations, and help to earn the respect and affection of the general public by giving demonstrations of trick riding, musical rides, and other exhibitions. Thus the horse can help the policeman in many ways.

The horse on film

Today's work horse can have more glamorous roles, although it is doubtful whether he appreciates it. The popularity of the Western movie, and the re-enactment of great battles on celluloid have produced a demand for film horses. Although this can be dangerous, as in the chariot race of *Ben Hur* when horses were actually killed, the majority of equine film stars are well cared for and trained.

The tourist horse

With rather speedier methods of transportation available than the horse the tourist trade has boomed. People are keen to see as much as possible of different countries and an increasingly popular form of holiday is the trek or trail ride. Equestrian centres are multiplying in picturesque parts of the world. They supply calm, tough horses and ponies that take the tourists for long rides, sometimes camping out at night, across beautiful and interesting country.

In old cities the carriage is returning, for tourist-orientated entrepreneurs have discovered that old fashioned horse-drawn cabs are a popular means of touring a city. The horse still has work to do but now with mechanical power available to perform the menial or hard tasks, he does have an easier and more enjoyable life.

Left: Canada's mounted policemen, the Mounties, are world famous and have performed their colourful musical ride in many countries. (*Robert Estall*)

Above: A British mounted policeman on duty controlling and directing the crowds at a horse show. (*Sylvester Jacobs*)

187

Index

Numbers in italics refer to illustrations